CW00594455

My Pe[arl]
of Great Price

Autobiography – Book I

Scotland to Uganda

Joo Hunty & Katie

Best Wishes

Edie Garvie

Edie Garvie

My Pearl of Great Price: Autobiography Book I

Copyright © Edie Garvie 2003

ISBN: 1 903607 42 6

All rights reserved. No part of this publication may be reproduced, stored in a retrieval system or transmitted in any form or by any means electronic, mechanical, photocopying or otherwise without the prior permission in writing of the copyright holder.

Typeset and published by:

Able Publishing
13 Station Road
Knebworth
Hertfordshire SG3 6AP

Tel: (01438) 814316/812320 Fax: (01438) 815232

Web: www.ablepublishing.co.uk
Email: fp@ablepublishing.co.uk

Contents

Foreword

It is with great delight and pleasure that I write a foreword to this wonderful account of Edie Garvie's life.

I first met Edie in the 1980s and since then she has been a great source of inspiration and support, both professionally and personally in my life.

This is the first of Edie's writings about her fascinating life, work and adventures. It is her multi-coloured journey of experiences, questioning, learning and teaching. As with all good journeys, some of the most important aspects are the means of transport, the places visited, the food along the way and the people met. This story of Edie's is full of amazingly different modes of transport, fascinating and vibrant places, tantalising descriptions of food and the most wonderful and interesting people – the most important of these, of course, being Edie herself!

One of Edie's books for teachers, which I have referred to a great deal in my own teacher training work, is called 'Story as Vehicle' in which she shows the reader how language can be taught through the vehicle of a story. In this, Edie's own story, you will find a wonderful vehicle in which we come to know and understand Edie herself in lots of different ways. It is a delight and fascination to see her thoughts and reflections as she grows up, has social experiences, travels and develops professionally. It is also quite a historically, politically and socially interesting account of one person's journey through the twentieth century and into the twenty-first, including war years.

On reflection I realise that all my encounters with Edie have involved journeys and lots of discussion and seeking of further understanding. This seems to epitomise what Edie is about – travelling, doing, questionning and talking all at the same time, with the odd bit of singing and acting thrown in!

I recall that when 'Story as Vehicle' was first published, we were in a taxi in London, going from King's Cross to a British Council meeting. Edie wrote some words for me in the front cover of a copy and gave it to me whilst we were talking about the meeting to come and discussing our recent work. And all this as we hung on to the straps, with the driver driving in an 'interesting' manner.

I felt I was paying homage to the essence of the contents of this book when I realised that the manuscript I'd been sent by Edie to read, travelled with me to many countries in lots of cars, trains, boats and planes. I do hope your copy does much travelling too.

I am sure you will enjoy the beginning of this story of Edie's life as much as I have – it's a *pearl* of a read from a *pearl* of a person.

Annie Hughes
Assistant Director EFL (English as a Foreign Language) Unit
University of York

June 2003

Introduction

A Quaker Reflects

I joined the Religious Society of Friends some years ago and have come to value highly the stillness in the Meeting for Worship. It has given a new dimension to my prayer-time at home. As a Christian I have always considered prayer to be important, an integral part of living, but now as I grow old and reflective I find that being still at some stage every day is essential. In a busy life of doing it allows one to be.

To quite a large extent this book is the outcome of my reflective prayer. Now in my mid seventies I have a great deal to be thankful for in a rich and varied life and I write to share it. It is of course possible to pray anywhere even for instance in the busy noise of an airport departure lounge. The degree of physical quietness is irrelevant when the mind is still. Nevertheless, it is helpful to have a special place at home where you can feel at rest, a place where past, present and future can meet in the Light of God's presence. This place for me is a favourite chair next to my sideboard in my living-room, with the middle drawer open.

The Middle Drawer

The souvenirs of my life are scattered about my home as they are with most people, things which evoke memories and a great surge of thankfulness. For me, the diaries, letters, photographs and newspaper cuttings in my study are a kind of focussing of all this but what is an even greater focussing is the content of this middle drawer of the sideboard, a set of icons as it were which reflects my total memorabilia. Here, over the years, I have collected items of special significance to me – certain letters, programmes and conference data, membership cards – reminders of particular events, achievements and failures – and much more. There is for instance a Bible and a copy of the Quaker 'Advices and Queries' along with other key books and prayer cards. There are selected greetings cards from close friends, a few of which I concentrate on each week so that all are covered constantly in prayer. It seems to me that the people behind the cards speak to me directly. Some things in the drawer change but most remain constant and provide a wonderful anchor to my wandering thoughts.

When the drawer is open I 'centre down' as the Quakers say, and 'hold in the light' people, places and situations – past, present and future. It is, I suppose, rather like clicking in to an era on screen with scenes coming into focus, fading and being replaced by others. It is a prayer strategy which I find calming and strengthening. All through my life I have been conscious of God's presence and empowering though not until now in my retirement from the fray and in the increasing reflection required for the writing of this book, have I been quite so aware and sure that we do not travel alone. The writing is my way of saying thank you to God and the hundreds of human beings in hundreds of places and situations through whom He has been present in my life. It is dedicated to them, and to all those who have helped me to find my pearl of great price.

"...the Kingdom of Heaven is like unto a merchant man seeking goodly pearls;
Who, when he had found one pearl of great price, went and sold all that he had, and bought it."

St Matthew 13: 45 and 46

About This Book

It is a cliché to speak of the journey of life but like all clichés it is meaningful or it would not be a cliché. I cannot avoid this one. In fact my reflections have indicated two main journeys, the professional and the spiritual, both progressing in the context of physical travel in Britain and in the wider world. Even my leisure-time activities seem to have had a pattern and a progression, one in particular becoming an almost full-time interest. I have found it exciting that the seeds of all this were planted very early, whether by nature or nurture or a combination of both. A scientist would explain it better. I see in my early years a kind of molecule waiting to be developed. This of course is true of every living being. I was especially fortunate in that so many of the atoms of this molecule were enabled to grow. I had the appropriate experience. Opportunities were manifold. I am only sorry that I did not always avail myself of them as I ought. I am very conscious of both the failures and the successes.

Be that as it may, the book is the first part of my story which friends have been urging me to write and which I started reluctantly and then began to enjoy. I have had a rich and very full life, not the 'normal' one of wife and mother but a life of service nonetheless, moving from a secure base to numerous ventures in many climes. I have much to be thankful for.

This first book covers my early life in Scotland and my years in Uganda in the service of Education. Broadly speaking it is chronological, the time-line being more marked in some parts than others. Sometimes I simply offer cameos to give an essence of the period. The closest members of my family and friends appear in these pages as valued companions on my journey. I only wish that time and space would have allowed for their stories to be told also. Perhaps this may be done elsewhere. And, so that my tale might be lodged in time I have endeavoured, as a kind of Greek Chorus, to touch on current events in the wider world.

But the book could not have been accomplished without the help of some special people. To all my family members and friends who listened, read, advised; to Cathy and Robbie who helped with the cover design; and to my 'boys' in Uganda and Ganesh nearer home for their stimulation of my Uganda memories – a huge thank you. My particular thanks to Annie for her foreword, to my brother Alex for his time-consuming reading and helpful comments and to Susan who took me into the 21st century with her computer typing and floppy disks, a constant support and companion from the start of the venture. Finally my thanks to 'Able' for their gentle guidance throughout and to those who urged me to write in the first place. My apologies for any sins of omission or commission.

Edie Garvie
Peterborough
July 2003

Part 1

The Scottish Years

1928 – 1960

'In my beginning is my end'

T S Eliot – Four Quartets, 'East Coker'

The Family

Scottish Background – The Garvie Family

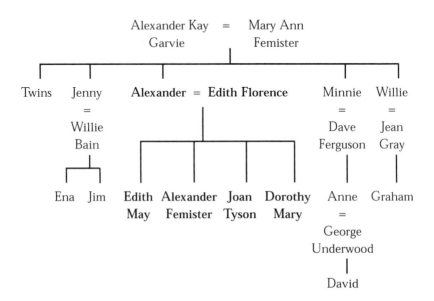

English Background – The Tyson Family

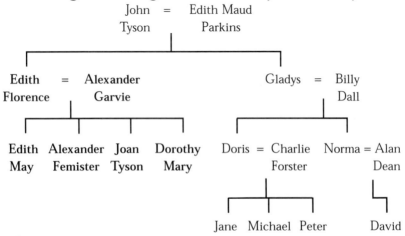

Those who appear in the family trees are within the scope of this book, except Gran's twins who died at birth. The 'trees' will be extended in later books as more family members marry and have children. By 1965, only Doris, Norma and Anne of my generation, wre married. The latter had her only child, Doris had all three of hers and Norma her first. The names given in the 'trees' are those used in the book. The central nuclear family is shown in bold print.

Grandparents

Alexander K. Garvie (Daddy's Daddy) was born in 1861 in Edinburgh. He became a printer there. Mary Ann Femister (Gran) was born in Nairn on the Moray Firth in 1866. She was in domestic service and her work took her to Edinburgh where she met Alexander. They were married in 1888. My father was born in Edinburgh in 1893.

John Tyson (Grandpa) was born in Kirkby-in-Furness in what is now Cumbria in 1875. Edith Maud (Grandma) was born (1869) in Yorkshire. The family moved to Manchester where John and Edith met and married in 1899. John was an engineer in the Post Office. My mother was born in Manchester in 1900, soon after which the family moved to Edinburgh where my mother was brought up, met my father and married him in 1925.

Chapter 1

The Early Years

My Beginning

It was the year 1928 when women in Britain got the vote. It was also the year of my birth. I wonder if this is significant. I have a feeling that had I been born twenty years earlier I might well have been a disciple of Emmeline Pankhurst! Perhaps my story will make this clear.

I first saw the light of day in a modest flat in the Blackhall district of Edinburgh. My parents were Edith and Alexander (Edie and Alex) and I was their first child. Father was a clerk in a brewer's office. We were not affluent but we were comfortable and I was much cherished. It must have been a terrible trauma when at the age of six months I nearly died. Aunts, uncles and grandparents were all called upon to share the onerous task of keeping me alive by pacing the floor with me night and day. I had whooping cough and I must not be allowed to lie down lest I whoop myself to death. That their efforts succeeded, this tale bears evidence. It is also, I suppose, an endeavour to convince myself that the Almighty was justified in allowing it!

Springvalley Gardens

Soon after this event we moved to the Morningside district, to a top flat of a tenement in Springvalley Gardens. We were to stay there until I was eight years old. When I was six my brother Alex was born in the nursing-home at 71, Great King Street where several years later my sisters Joan and Dorothy were also born. So for the first six years of my life I was an only child enjoying all the love and care of my young parents. At the same time I made full use of my lively imagination and created imaginary playmates. More of this below. What follows now are a few cameos from these years, in Glasgow as well as Edinburgh. My maternal grandparents lived in Glasgow at that time though they later moved to Edinburgh again. There was much visiting in both directions.

Country Memories

We were in Juniper Green, Mother, Dad and a three-year-old me. It was a Saturday walk in the country just outside Edinburgh, an area to the south of the city which was to become a source of many fond memories but on this occasion my recollection is one of shock and tears. Rushing to see the hens in a farm I fell on the gravel and grazed my knee. It was not serious nor did it hurt very much and all was well till I saw the red patch, probably the first time I had seen my own blood! How I yelled and continued to do so all the way back into Edinburgh on the bus. We got off in the High Street. I remember being carried on my father's shoulders, still crying and feeling sorry for myself, as we went for the 23 tramcar which would take us to Gran's. Every crisis, real or imaginary seemed to be resolved at Gran's and I am sure this one was.

Another picture which comes into memory's focus is the Braidburn Valley. My mother would take me on a sunny afternoon. In the early thirties this was a very rural scene, the Braid Hills dominant and today's built-up area yet to be. It was, still is, a pretty place with its stream, or

In the Braidburn Valley

burn as we call it in Scotland, running through the sloping fields on its way to join the Water of Leith. There was a path along the top of the fields on one side of the valley. Here my mother would find a bench or sit on the grass while I played. A favourite game was shops. I would collect flowers and grasses, sort them out in bundles and lay out my stall. Mother was my customer. How I loved role-playing and even at a very early age I could live happily for long periods in the land of my imagination.

More Imaginative Play

My bedroom in the Springvalley Gardens flat is the next venue which comes to mind. My bedhead consisted of a number of wooden slats. Lying awake for a long time as I often did both at night and in the early morning, I made these posts became my playmates. I gave them names but I ran out of ideas and then had big Jean and little Jean and big Mary and little Mary. Once I started school these girls were the pupils in my class and I of course was the teacher.

Grandma's house in Glasgow was another place of fertile imaginative play. I can see so clearly the squared pattern of the wall-paper in the passage which led to the kitchen. One of the squares was the doorbell for my house, Grandma's kitchen quarters. And in my bedroom in this house the patterns on the net-curtains on the window were animals in some exotic land. I used to lie awake and invent stories of the curtain creatures. I roamed and ventured far beyond my room, no doubt the adventures tinged with my day-time walks with Grandpa particularly to see the ships on the Clyde and the strange trees in the Fossil Grove in Victoria Park. They had turned to stone in their longevity. Little did I know that some of these exotic wanderings in my Glasgow bedroom were to become very real in my future life.

Even later, when I was no longer an only child, I still indulged in imaginary companions. For instance I had a particular doll, Marie, around whom I wove a whole life of home and school. I realise now that much of what I imagined was a projection of my own longings. Marie was my daughter. She did many of the things I longed to do, the non-conforming things like wearing non-uniform to school. Was this an early indication of my 'rebel' nature? I always enjoyed shocking people out of unthinking convention and complacency. I wanted to know why I should do things but wasn't supposed to question.

Then there were my two 'friends', Margaret Barclay and Beryl Dawson. They lived in a road off Morningside Drive. Now, in my seventies, I still look for their houses when I am in the area. Margaret always wore neat school uniform. She attended a school I aspired to and always pleased her parents and teachers. She had mousy, straight hair and was very dull. Beryl on the other hand attended my school, was a tomboy who flouted the rules, had red curly hair and got up to all sorts of exciting ploys.

A Red-letter day

I must have been about four when my imaginings were stimulated further by a very special day. We were staying with my grandparents in Glasgow. My father took me into the centre of the city. The first wonderful thing was the tramride. Grandpa had his own car and I was not used to the Glasgow trams which seemed different from the Edinburgh ones. In particular they were distinguished by the broad band of colour round the vehicle depicting which route they travelled. I think we were on the red tram. We sat upstairs, another novelty. I became conscious for the first time of the 'funny' way people spoke in Glasgow, somehow different from the way we did in Edinburgh. I also noticed the colour of the buildings. They were pink. Those in Edinburgh were grey. This really was an adventure.

Emerging in central Glasgow we went into a large store, probably Marks and Spencer. There was counter after counter of wonderful things. I was too little to see properly but then my father lifted me up at the place of teddy-bears. I had a much-loved teddy at home which had once been of the conventional yellowish beige and was now somewhat the worse for wear. He was known as Foostie. What drew my eyes out on stalks at this counter was the welter of colour. Heaps and heaps of teddies, blue, green, pink – every colour imaginable – were on display, each with a contrasting coloured ribbon round its neck.

When I was asked to choose one for myself my excitement knew no bounds. I was lost for words and paralysed for action. Then I moved. I took a pink teddy with a green bow. He was named Fluffy and he was my close companion for the next two big events of the day. Looking back now I see Fluffy as an important symbol in my life. He represented difference. For me up to that point teddy-bears were beige. I had just discovered that they could be other colours and the knowledge made me very happy. Different but valid and lovely. How important this concept was to become for me!

The next vivid memory is having a meal in a restaurant, another first. I have no recollection of what I ate, only of the wonder of sitting at the table in this vast room full of tables, with Fluffy on my lap. I was in a new exciting world. But greater was to follow. I found myself after lunch in the dark and mysterious depths of a cinema, or picture-house as it was called then. The film was set in a zoo and a curly-haired boy was shut in after the gates were locked for the night. I don't remember him coming to any harm nor how the story finished, but I do recall my feelings of empathy with this boy as he searched in vain for his parents and realised he would have to share the hours of darkness with the animals. Again Fluffy sat on my lap and my father was near, to protect in case it all became too much, sitting in a darkened theatre with only the occasional flash of light from the usherette's torch. I had been transported into someone else's world. It was scary but I loved it. The terrors were quickly lost in pleasurable interest and I was beginning to enjoy the unknown. It was the start of a lifelong passion for the exotic.

Lost and Found

However there was an occasion when my new-found spirit of adventure led me into trouble. It was a lovely warm day and we were all in Grandma's garden, the adults dozing after lunch in a tent and I playing outside it. A girl whom I knew came by. She was a little older than I. Would I like to go to the shops with her? Of course I would and I went, never thinking to inform my parents. We had to cross the wide, busy Dumbarton Road. This we safely did, two small girls hand in hand. I cannot remember much about the shopping but what happened next is very clear. My companion said she had to go off somewhere else and could I manage home alone? I waved her off cheerfully and recrossed the Dumbarton Road safely. Then the trouble began. I was faced with a number of parallel roads which all looked very much alike. Grandma lived in one of them but which? I chose the wrong one. I went to where I expected the house to be and it wasn't. The world fell apart!

I stood in the middle of the street (there seemed to be no traffic at all in these side streets), a forlorn little figure in tartan skirt and white blouse, and I howled. My crying attracted two good ladies who took me in hand, for God was surely with me. All I could give by way of address was my home in Edinburgh. I had not memorised that of my grandparents and could only speak of Grandpa Jack. So my new friends walked me around the area, presumably hoping that something would be familiar to me. They bought me biscuits when I said I was hungry; asked the advice of a policeman on the beat, during which I ran off! But they caught up with me again and we continued our perambulations.

Meantime my family had informed the police that I was missing. My father and grandfather were circling round in the car and Grandma, Mother and Grandma's friend Agnes were walking around the area. It was they who found me. They turned a corner and there I was, a hand in each of my protector's. Later, in the house, I was amazed to see my mother weeping. I am supposed to have said, 'I don't know why Mummy is crying. It was me that was lost.' With the innocence of the four-year-old I had no idea of the damage I had caused. My poor mother suffered a horrendous miscarriage and was very ill for some time. When she was recovering it was deemed necessary for her to have a holiday and a change of scene.

We went to a cottage in Aberdour, a little seaside town in Fife, on the other side of the Firth of Forth from Edinburgh. We were there for a month while my father commuted by train to his work. Mother and I met him every evening at the station. How I hated the dashing monster which was the steam-engine! I had to be kept in the waiting-room until the train had stopped and the great hissing, puffing creature had come to rest. A lasting memory of Aberdour is the night-mare I had one night. A great roaring beast was rushing to devour me and I woke up screaming just as the jaws were upon me. Needless to say I ended up in bed with my parents. I must have been a sore trial at times.

But there are happy memories of this time. There were lovely beaches, particularly the one known as the Silver Sands. My mother would play with me there or sit and read while I built sand-castles and enjoyed my usual imaginative games. Always a dreamer and player of roles, I was never at a loss. I was a strange mixture of imaginative fears and bold adventuring. This was to be a strand going through my life.

Early Dancing Days

I began to dance almost as soon as I could walk. When there was music on the wireless (I remember Henry Hall's programme in particular and can still hum the signature tune) I was always up and away. So I was taken to a dancing class. Miss Comfort held this in a large room of her house. My formless prancings were disciplined. I took part in two concerts in the Music Hall, first as a daisy being woken by the sun along with my fellow daisies and then as a butterfly in a duet. I remember trying to clamber up on to the stage from the auditorium instead of from the wings, much to the amusement of the audience and the embarrassment of my mother. Things were not going fast enough for me! But I loved performing. School stopped this dancing class but in a year or two I began a class in school itself and all through my life dancing was to have a big part.

The Butterfly

A Cocoon of Caring

In my only child days I was spoilt by all my relatives. They brought me innumerable presents. Certain of those stand out in my memory, the beautiful doll whom I called Jean, lovingly dressed by Gran, the thick pencil case containing every imaginable item in preparation for school brought by Grandma and Grandpa and all the mysterious gifts left by Mabel, my mother's cousin. Mabel was full of fun. She hid her presents all over the house and I found them after she had left, many of them in the vicinity of the piano which she loved to play. Mabel, music and secret gifts all go together.

The days when Grandma and Grandpa came from Glasgow to visit were high days and holidays. Not only did they bring me a present but there was always a ride somewhere in Grandpa's car. Grandma was a tiny lady with a scent of lavender about her. In her fur coat she looked like a small penguin. Grandpa seemed to me to be a huge man. I was slightly in awe of him. He and Grandma were a somewhat incongruous pair but I loved them.

Gran came every Saturday afternoon after visiting Daddy's Daddy in the hospital which was very near. She too came bearing gifts. Sometimes she came before her hospital visit and took me to see my grandfather but my memories of this are very vague. What I do remember well are walks with Gran when she revealed to me her country woman's knowledge of the flowers and grasses which then grew in profusion in the hedgerows. She imbued in me a love of the countryside and what I can only describe as a sense of the sacred in the ordinary.

Then of course there were the aunts and uncles and cousins Ena and Jim. There was much visiting back and forth, Auntie Gladys in particular helping me to go to sleep at night. She was my godmother. Jim and I became very close and I began to look upon him as an elder brother. He even took me to football matches! But I never became an addict. My life in these early years revolved around the Springvalley flat, the homes of my closest relatives, my dancing class and the Sunday-school. It was a very cosy, sheltered existence in the midst of a troubled world and the strident shouts of the newsboys on the street corners. Hitler was in the headlines and Europe was beginning the run-up to war. Meantime for me, there was my playmate, Oliv (I never did discover why her name had no 'e' at the end) and the street culture and there was my first real adventure story.

Oliv and the Street Culture

Oliv lived in a flat opposite. We were four years old when we met in the street, the same height, both with short hair and a fringe. I was very fair and Oliv dark, almost swarthy. Her birthday was the day before mine. We became fast friends and eventually started school together. Oliv was allowed to play in the street and it was only with much pleading that I was permitted to join her. My parents were wary, even in those days, of letting me loose. The top floor flat was a long way up and it was difficult for my mother to find me quickly once I had gone to play.

So in some ways I was deprived of the street culture. I was not allowed to play out very much, only with Oliv and Evelyn, another girl who lived opposite and went to a posh fee-paying school! My parents were particularly doubtful about the children who lived in Springvalley Terrace, a street which ran into the Gardens and bisected our side. They were unaware that Oliv and I did join the gang for a while until one of the boys took liberties with me in a rather dark entry. It gave me a fright but had no lasting effect except to confirm my mother's warning and make me a little more careful. Nevertheless I felt somehow that I was missing out on something, especially the picture house at the end of the Gardens. There were serial movies running there on Saturday mornings. Payment I believe was by jam-jar. Oliv went, and related to me the stories of the films but I was not allowed to go.

The Night the Boiler Burst

In 1934 and two weeks before my sixth birthday my brother Alex was born. This made a huge difference to my life as I hope to show as my story unfolds. I mention it now because Alex was a part of the adventure of the boiler, if only in a supporting role. It was a wintry, stormy night. My father had gone to visit Gran as he did at least once every week and Mother and baby Alex and I were snug in the flat, the curtains drawn against the warring elements. I played with my doll in the kitchen living-room and put her to bed while my mother did the same with her real live doll in the bedroom next door.

The kitchen was very quiet save for the ticking of the clock and the wind rattling the window and moaning in the chimney where Auld Nick (Scottish name for the devil) lived. I remember moving more into the centre of the room. The fireplace seemed redolent with the things in nightmares. I was on the point of joining my mother in the bedroom when she returned and all was well. Then it happened. There was a little pop like the sound of a cork coming out of a bottle and water began to trickle into the fire. By the look on my mother's face I could see that this should not be happening and my belief that the devil lived behind the fire was confirmed. The fire went out and I was despatched to fetch a bucket and cloth while my mother stemmed the tide like the Dutch boy at the dyke by putting her finger in the hole. The boiler had burst.

None of this I really understood at the time, only that all was not as it should be and that my mother was very upset. The next thing I remember is rushing down our tenement stairs into the dark street and running along the Gardens to Morningside Road and the tramstop. I had to go to Gran's to fetch my father. Mother could not leave the baby or the boiler. This was an enormous adventure for a six-year old and my mother would never have allowed it if she had not been desperate. There was no telephone and no other way of reaching help.

Even in those days of comparatively dangerless streets my journey caused a few raised eyebrows. First a policeman on his beat came to talk to me as I stood at the tramstop. My garbled explanation of why I was out on my own and where I was going did not seem to satisfy him but he saw me on to the tram and exchanged some words with the conductor while I went inside and settled myself near the conductor's platform. The tram was the familiar 23. My mother had given me a penny for my fare and I proudly tendered it now. I was actually beginning to enjoy myself. Even the stares, muttered comments and some kindly smiles of my fellow passengers excited me. I found that I liked playing this strange new role. The mixture of apprehension and challenge seemed to agree with me.

The conductor kept a friendly eye on me. At one stage he said, 'Dinna lose yer ticket hen'. The inspector was coming on at The Mound and would want to see it. Apprehension took over again. Who or what was an inspector? Was Auld Nick still after me? But the inspection proved harmless. The route, what I could see of it in the dark and through the misted window, was one I recognised. We went past Bruntsfield Links and the King's Theatre, round by Tollcross and past the huge infirmary where sick people went and so on down The Mound.

The inspector's visit over we crossed Princes Street and headed for Canonmills by way of Hanover and Pitt Streets. Not all these names were known to me then but I knew the places, though the stormy darkness made them difficult to recognise. The conductor kept asking me if I knew where I was and where I was going. I assured him that I did in order to assure myself! Then I saw it, the little shop down some steps at the corner of Cumberland Street. The conductor must have been very relieved when I announced that I wanted off. I am surprised, looking back, that he did not get off with me and see me across the street but I suppose he had his schedule to keep and maybe I exuded a degree of confidence I did not altogether feel.

So I had to negotiate the wide street myself. There were two sets of tramlines to cross and nobody about to help. Luckily there seemed to be no traffic. It was not a night for anyone to be out if it was not necessary. I reached the corner shop safely. It was shuttered and dark. I crossed the end of the back mews and was soon at the entrance to Gran's tenement. She too lived in a top flat. I did not fancy plunging into the dimly-lit entry with its spooky passage leading to the back-green. Who knew what kind of bogey-men hovered in wait? But first I must climb these few outside steps and then try to ring the bell as I had seen my father do. Edinburgh tenement flats had their bells at the street door and had to be polished regularly with brasso. The name of the tenant was above the bell. I was too little to reach the top bell easily but standing on my toes and pulling with all my six-year-old might, I just managed a tiny ring.

How well I remember that climb to safety and mission accomplished, first the street door banging shut behind me and a black gulf absorbing me while my eyes and nostrils gradually got used to the gaslight coming from the next two floors. Then, with a wary glance in the direction of the back-green passage, I felt my way up the first flight of stairs towards the welcome and – joy of joys – the voice of Gran. I had no breath to answer her queries. I remember hearing her say in an astonished voice, 'It's the bairn'. No doubt she added the familiar 'Come away' which was her normal welcome. Then I reached the top landing and there she was with my father behind her. They were silhouetted against the brighter gaslight of the flat. I was tearful. Reaction had set in. I had done it and my responsibility was over. I have no recollection at all of how the boiler saga was resolved but resolved it must have been as life went on and I learned not to fear the devil behind the fireplace.

Chapter 2

The Braids

Two More Years at Springvalley Gardens

I had started school in the autumn of 1933 just before Alex was born – two traumatic events in my life. I went to James Gillespie's High School for girls, a stately edifice on the Bruntsfield Links and within walking distance of home. My mother had also attended this school and my sisters were to do so later. Like so many Edinburgh schools it was the result of philanthropical endowment. James Gillespie had been a snuff merchant. Even though the school came under the jurisdiction of the Edinburgh municipality the parents were charged a nominal fee for some reason. Did this raise us slightly above the 'ordinary' schools?! A particular claim to fame is that the film – 'The Prime of Miss Jean Brodie' – was based on our school. The prototype of Jean Brodie was a teacher in my time though I was never in her class. Muriel Spark, the writer of the book, was just ahead of me at school. Like other schools in the city Gillespie's had both primary and secondary departments. You moved into the higher grade in the same institution. I was there from the age of five until I was seventeen.

For two years I was an 'infant' with Miss Hay whom I dearly loved. I well remember when the new block was opened, housing a department for the youngest children. As monitor wearing an orange badge, I proudly led my classmates to our new room. It was an exciting day. As I write, the scents – new wood – plants – chalk, and the songs and music of the games, absorb me still. I shared all this with Oliv with whom I walked to and from school. For those two years we were inseparable. Oliv told me all about those movies I never went to, usually on our leisurely walk home. She was an enthusiastic raconteur of the adventures of Ken Maynard and Buck Jones.

My lonely childhood had changed and I revelled in it. Alex or Alexander Femister, to give him his full name, became my companion and pal at a very early age and before long I couldn't really remember not having him there. I have no recollection of feeling resentful or jealous, possibly because I still had my dream-life and was not dependent on my parents' attention. As a family, now of four, we continued our life in Springvalley Gardens, I 'helping' to look after my little brother with whom I began to share more and more.

Church and Sunday-school

A big influence in my life was church and Sunday-school. We went to College Church, Presbyterian and part of the Church of Scotland. It was near the university on the south side of Edinburgh, a very old establishment which my family on my father's side had attended over the generations. It was the place where my parents were married and we were all baptised. We went to Sunday-school with Ronnie Corbett, the well-known comedian. His family too had a long connection with the church. The church and all the relationships were like an extended family. We shared so much and not only on Sundays. As I grew up I went through Brownies, Guides and Girls' Association. I taught in the Sunday-school and sang in the choir. I even sat on the Congregational Board which looked after the property. My father was an elder and as a family we were an accepted and respected part of the rich congregational life. I give thanks for the fostering I received and the start it gave to my spiritual journey.

A Typical Sunday

And speaking of journeys, I cannot leave the topic of church without some mention of my walk to and from it and the whole ethos of Sunday for me as a child. It began with a large cooked breakfast, porridge followed by bacon and egg and numerous accompaniments. This was to set us up for the long morning ahead. It would be some time before we had lunch. The service did not end until 12.30 and for the children Sunday-school took another hour. While we lived in Springvalley Gardens we went by tram some of the way and then had what was for me a fascinating walk through the poor area in which the church was situated.

This was where my father had lived as a boy. The place had much deteriorated from its respectable working-class status. I was so interested in my father's stories of his boyhood games in the network of alleys around those streets. There were many getaway routes which the adults did not pursue. Like most children at play Dad and his chums got up to all kinds of mischief and then quickly disappeared down one of the many passages running through the tenements from street to back-green. The Empire Theatre was very near and Gran took in actors as lodgers. This subject also provided grist to the mill of Dad's tales with a richness which as a child I did not always understand! He had acquired a certain view of the theatre which was to have some effect on my career but more of that later. By the time I was on the scene the place was virtually a slum. I can vividly remember women, barefoot, with shawls serving as coats and very often a baby cuddling within the shawl. The children were barefoot too as they ran with jugs to the nearest pub of which there were many, to collect a gill of something. This was regular practice. I have often wondered what my father's thoughts were as he steered his respectable family through these scenes of his childhood now so changed, though the gaslight was still there and the paper-boy calling from his street-corner stance.

Another memory is that of the nuns we always seemed to meet at roughly the same point on our walk. The times of our respective services must have coincided. They wore dark blue habits and huge white head-dresses. They were full of mystery and rather frightening. Nobody wanted to or perhaps could not explain to me the phenomenon of these strange catholics! But the place where we met was of much more interest. It always seemed to be outside a sweet shop which was open on Sundays! The 'pokes' of rock I can still visualise, stowed away until after lunch and the contents much enjoyed.

After church and Sunday-school we walked to Gran's. The adults had gone on ahead. Lunch and tea at the Cumberland Street flat was also a very important part of the Sunday ritual as was the long walk with our tummies rumbling, from College Church on the south side to Gran's, right away across Princes Street and into the 'new' town to the north. It really was quite a marathon. In those early years there were three of us, my cousins Ena and Jim and myself but quite soon Alex was also able to join us. The streets were wonderfully free of traffic, especially on a Sunday, and it was easy crossing roads even for children. Once across Princes Street, Edinburgh's elegant centre, we were soon on our way towards our destination. Hanover Street slopes up towards George Street another fine road which runs parallel to Princes Street. On topping this rise one can see, on a good day, right across the Firth of Forth to Fife. It is a stupendous view. But I see this now with adult eyes. At the time of which I write we children were more concerned with reaching Cumberland Street and the appetising lunch we knew Gran would have for us. There was always broth, even in summer, followed by roast beef, roast potatoes and boiled and other vegetables and then plum pudding and fruit and custard. The adults were already out for the count and had begun to doze over the 'Sunday Post', a popular Scottish Sunday paper which is still going. Features called 'Oor Wullie' and 'The Broons' we all enjoyed, even the adults. There was great competition to be the first to acquire these. If the weather was fine we were soon dispatched to the Botanic gardens, again on foot and if wet, to the museum. But we were allowed to play for a little while in the sitting-room with its smoky fire. This was a large room with two windows and a small box bedroom off. I can still smell the smoke from the fire, mingled with the moth balls.

The same room in the flat below was rented from the Leitch family there by Gran's two sisters, Teen and Jessie, and always after tea and just before we left for home we had to visit the 'aunties'. More scent of moth-balls but also of lavender, long black frocks and lots of lace. The aunties were older than Gran, and still lived in the Edwardian age. They sat, one in each window, two old ladies caught in a time warp, as we dutifully paid our call. Teen was blind and gently reached out to touch us. Others in the Cumberland Street scene were Auntie Jenny who came only for tea and to collect Ena and Jim. For some reason neither she nor her husband went to church but Ena and Jim were regulars. They shared our pew, attended Sunday-school and were part of the whole Sunday scene at Gran's. Uncle Willie and Auntie Jean came from Portobello occasionally and Auntie Minnie and Uncle Dave from Kelso. We would play with cousin Anne, a year older than Alex. Even Mother's side of the family would join us sometimes. Then there were the lodgers, usually a lady in the back room and a gentleman in the front one near the door. There was a Mrs Bell I recall who was very generous with sweets. She wore an enormous hat. The kitchen was the focus of all this activity, the snug centre of the family in more ways than one. Gran lived in this room. She had the box-bedroom off it as her bedroom and a favourite chair beside the range fireplace where she sat in the evenings and dispensed wisdom. There was a stool next to the chair. How often I sat there and shared things with Gran, almost until the day she died in 1956 when I was twenty eight. Gran had very little formal education but she had wonderful understanding and could come straight to the heart of a matter. We all owe her a great deal. There is so much more I could say about this meaningful, influential strand in my young life but perhaps there is enough here to give a flavour not only of 'Sunday' but of the whole aura which was Gran.

Braid Road

In 1936 we moved to a flatted villa in Braid Road near the Braid Hills which became a favourite playground for Alex and me. We had secret passages amongst the whins, the Scottish name for gorse.There was even a shallow cave which centred largely in our play. This place is full of memories and will appear again in my story. We revelled in our garden. Alex and I each had our own patch, marked off with stones. In mine was a tree which was covered in orange berries in the autumn, inhabited by a colony of bees I considered as my pets. I loved my bee tree. And just over the wall lived Morag, a tomboyish redhead about my own age who rapidly became a playmate. Our two gardens formed a land of new adventure. For Alex and me these were years of close companionship which was greatly enhanced not only by our play but also by our walks. We were sent for 'messages', a Scottish word for shopping. It was quite a long walk either down the hill to the shops in Comiston Road or up the way to what were known then as the new shops in the developing area of Fairmilehead. There was not much traffic about, the place was not yet built up, and it was safe for children to wander about and enjoy the country air and wide open spaces. We chatted about so many things and I started my teaching career with my little brother who was an avid learner and a future professor of Greek.

During the first two years at Braid Road I met Mairi. We were in the same class at Gillespie's and she took the place of Oliv who had moved to a different class. I think that of all my chums Mairi was the one to whom I best related over many years. We shared so much. We were both in the school dancing class, chosen to dance once in a concert in the ill-fated Theatre Royal. It was burned down not long after. I

Eighth bithday party in the garden of the Braid Road house.
The tall girl, centre back, is cousin Ena. Edie is in front of her with Oliv on
Edie's left. Sitting, front left, is cousin Doris with sister Norma on her right.
Centre front is neighbour, Morag, and the only boy is Alex.

cannot remember if there were any fatalities but I think of that warren of passages and I shudder to imagine what might have happened to anyone caught there. At nine years of age I was thrilled to be dancing in a real theatre. At about the same time I took a small part in a play produced by a family friend who ran a dramatic society. The smell of grease-paint, the tummy butterflies while waiting in the wings, the footlights and the thrill of performing – never left me till the end of my days. For now this was something I enjoyed with Mairi.

I also have wonderful memories of play on the Pentland Hills just south of Edinburgh and of going with Mairi's family to Hundleshope Farm near Peebles where they had a caravan. There the border hills became our haunt where we roamed and talked. How we talked, even about current world events, young as we were! The rumble of war was getting closer. Mairi was a Macdonald of highland stock, a strong personality and a quiet anchor for the ebullient and somewhat impulsive character which was me.

Pre-war Memories

In those pre-war years, school continued normally. I had of course to travel by tram as our new home was much farther away from the school. The fare was a penny (old money) for school children. Some mornings I went into school early. I attended the Scripture Union meetings held in the art-room. My interest in the Bible grew apace with that of the theatre! Maybe there is more connection than one would expect!

Another pungent memory is the annual holiday. In my very early years this was spent in Largs on the Firth of Clyde. We took 'digs' with an estate-worker's family called Lightbody at Netherhall. The walled garden with its goldfish pond and the scent of flowers, especially the phlox, come vividly to mind, also the loft in the old stable where I romped with the Lightbody children. But the most exciting recollection

Class of 1937-38. Edie is in the second front row, the rebel with different coloured socks! Mairi is third from left in the third row.

is the sailing on the Clyde steamers, specially the late-night one when lots of ships converged on Rothesay Bay and the sky was lit up with fireworks. Even more enthralling for me were the visits to the 'Entertainers', summer shows whose actors went on, many of them, to higher things. Both of these events were a kind of fairyland. The screaming of gulls and the scent of seaweed can still touch off the impressions gained in these formative years when the Largs holiday was such a huge item in the family agenda.

Later we went to Nairn instead. I don't know why. Perhaps the Lightbodys stopped taking lodgers. We had two, or was it three, holidays here, a pleasant seaside town on the Moray Firth, famous for its many hours of sunshine and its lovely sandy beach. Again we went into lodgings as the custom was in those days. We bought our own supplies and the landlady cooked for us. We were with the Russells, a large family with whom we became very involved and felt much at home. There was a child, Emma, who played happily with Alex and me in the long sloping garden of the two-storeyed house. We had a sitting-room and bedroom on the ground floor. How well I remember the awful flooding one year and everyone recruited to move our belongings and most of the furniture to the floor above! I have a treasure-house of recollections, the gorgeous black spaniel puppies bred by one of the Russells and entered for the Nairn Show, the coming of the fair on the links and the excitement of discovering in the morning what my parents had won on the 'lucky number' stall. On one occasion I became the proud possessor of a large rabbit in plush velvet suit with great white floppy ears and Alex had Marvel, his much-loved dog. We watched the fishermen in their wooden huts by the harbour where they smoked their herring, spread out on racks over fires made with fir-cones. The Nairn speldings were very special. When we took some once to blind Auntie Teen in Edinburgh she immediately said, 'Nairn speldings'. They smelled and tasted like no other smoked fish.

But perhaps the memory of Nairn I value most is that of the little school just over the wall from where we lived. By a strange co-incidence we had come next to the very school which Gran attended till she was twelve, before going into service. She had fascinated me with her tales of her school-days, particularly her walk of two miles to and from Auld

Earn. In winter the snow was sometimes so deep that she had to walk on top of the dyke, the word used in Scotland, as in the Netherlands, for 'wall'. And here it was, the place of Gran's tales. My imagination ran rife.

Our last Nairn holiday was in 1938 when I was ten. Mother was expecting my sister Joan who was born in October. The birth of my sister was a very exciting event, especially as she was so different. Unlike Alex and myself who were blond, Joan was dark with lovely large eyes. I longed for her to grow up so that I could share sisterly matters with her but for a long time Joan was more of a live doll than a companion as I helped my mother to care for her.

The year 1938 was that of the Glasgow Exhibition in Bella Houston Park. Once again it was an exciting day out for me and my father. The most exhilarating event was the ride on the big dipper. Dad and I were in the front seat so first over the edge. Behind us was a group of Boy Scouts whose shrieks affected everyone else. Dad held on to me firmly as I tended to rise from the seat, clutching the rail in front, while I screamed in concert with the boys behind.

The Exhibition memories are many, much walking and pushing through crowds, huge tented pavilions with goods of every conceivable kind being advertised and offered for sale. I remember being highly amused when Dad was 'caught' by a sales lady on a perfume stall. He was made to sample several of her wares. Greatly discomfited he bought something for Mother and we made our escape. We also managed to buy a special toy for Alex. That Easter we had been to Grandma and Grandpa's as usual and Alex and I had been playing in the garden. Alex had left his prized fire-engine out and when he went to retrieve it it had disappeared. He was so upset and I was too. Anything hurting Alex hurt me. We never did recover the fire-engine but we were able to replace it.

The clouds of war were rolling towards us. I understood something of the depression, unemployment, Hitler and the Munich appeasement. My day in Glasgow at the exhibition is about the last big pre-war event I can remember. I was caught up in the frenetic activity of a society trying desperately to assure itself of the security of the future and business as usual. By late summer of the following year we were at war.

War and Evacuation to Kelso

War was declared on 3rd September 1939. I was eleven and in the last year of my primary school. Alex was five and just about to start school. Children all over the country were being sent out of the cities for safety. At first I was to have gone to distant relations in California but when the evacuee ship, City of Benares, was torpedoed with very few survivors, my parents decided we should all remain together. My mother and Alex and Joan and I went to Kelso to stay with Auntie Minnie and Uncle Dave. Their daughter Anne was six and a good playmate especially for Alex. She was proud to help him settle in at school. The novelty for me was having boys in my class. I also made two interesting discoveries. One was how hopeless I was at knitting and the other that I had a pleasant singing voice. We had a very musical headmaster and when I sang to my parents the carols he was teaching us they were delighted, especially Dad who had been a chorister in St Mary's Cathedral in Edinburgh.

Uncle Dave became the Provost of this delightful Borders town and the family lived in a large quaint old house on the banks of the River Tweed very close to the bridge and the ancient abbey. We were there for four months. My father stayed with Gran while he continued in his job, and came to us at the weekend. We had wonderful hospitality and kindness in Kelso, even a sitting-room and bedroom to ourselves, but it could not have been easy for my mother and Auntie Minnie sharing a kitchen, nor for Mother coping with the three of us in restricted accommodation. I personally loved that time. It was a beautiful autumn and we children roamed the countryside finding conkers under the horse-chestnut trees. I even learned to ride a bicycle there. In the house also were John and Ena, evacuees from an Edinburgh school and about my own age. Mr Inglis, the Baptist minister who lodged with my aunt and uncle, took us all in hand, the children that is. He formed us into a kind of club and organised all kinds of exciting activities for us. This must have been a great relief to our parents.

My father's weekly visit was a highlight, not only for his own family. He arrived on Saturday afternoon and left on Sunday evening, travelling by bus. On the journey home the vehicle had to crawl through the newly-imposed blackout. It must have been very tedious for the passengers. Dad's suitcase was always full of goodies. All the children were remembered and we waited breathlessly to see what he had in store. Sweets, story and colouring books, pencils and crayons etc. were duly dispensed. The shortages in the shops had not yet begun and Dad, unlike most men, liked shopping. It gave him great pleasure to choose these gifts and to see us so happy with them. I remember that time in Kelso with warm affection as I revelled in the new experience and in playing yet another role, that of evacuee. But it was not to last. When it was seen that Edinburgh was not apparently an important enemy target we returned home. This was just before Christmas.

More about Kelso

But I cannot move on without pausing to linger a little longer in Kelso. I was to return many times and I never lost my early love for the place. The central square has been compared with a French 'place'. It was cobbled in my childhood and still is. One of the famous views for postcards of the town is that of the bridge over the River Tweed with the ruined abbey to the right on the town side. Some of the postcards show a row of houses to the left of the bridge and close to the river. It was in the middle one of these that my aunt and uncle lived. The houses were very old, all communicating in a strange L shape. There was a large communal garden fronting the river with a wooden gate on to Belmont Place, another interesting cobbled square which contained St Andrew's Episcopal church and, of particular interest when we were children, Katie Bennet's sweet-shop. This was an Aladdin's cave of treasure in tall glass bottles which sat amongst the dust! Both Katie in her old-fashioned garb and her tiny shop were greatly loved.

In the wartime absence of traffic Belmont Place was a peaceful backwater. Sometimes fishermen would make their way down to the river by a path at the end of the church. There was a ford here where stonework of the original bridge could be seen. The primary school which I attended very briefly lies behind the abbey still. It is now a community centre. I have memories of soldiers coming to requisition it and of us being taken to church halls, but I have a special memory of the family dog Sandy following me to school and of the teacher Miss Scott, giving me some string to put round his collar so I could lead him home.

Another special memory of that time is the Bible Class dance. I felt very grown up. Bible class was a step up from Sunday-school. Ena and I looked forward to the event for weeks. I had left my mother's bedroom and was now sharing Ena's attic room. We laid out our dresses for the dance a long time in advance along with shoes and other accessories, the most exciting being our first silk stockings. Ena's ensemble was yellow; mine was pink. I remember much more about the preparations than about the dance itself. And speaking of dances, Auntie Minnie and Uncle Dave organised them for the troops. I was allowed to go when I was in my early teens. This was yet another exciting experience. I had some handsome partners including Polish officers. We had many nationals of other European countries in our forces during the war, those who had escaped the Hitler invasions, some of whom lodged with my aunt and uncle.

Although only a small market town, Kelso is a lively community and it played its part well in the war years. My cousin Anne, married to George and now a grandmother, lives there yet, her pleasant home in a newer developed area of the town. I enjoy visiting. We often go to Floors Castle, seat of the Duke of Roxburgh – which is open to the public. In addition to Kelso's scenic attractions it has much of historic importance. There are the remains of the ancient castle of Roxburgh just across the Tweed from Floors, all that is left of the old town. Then of course there is the abbey, one of a number in the Borders built by King David. Kelso was founded in 1128. But I begin to sound like a guide book. Before I get lost in the interest and beauty of one of my favourite places, I must return to Edinburgh.

Back to Edinburgh

We now paused for breath as it were, and inevitably stayed at Gran's over Christmas and New Year 1940, Gran, as always, good for crisis resolution. I remember walking with Mum and Dad and Alex along the pier at Granton on a beautiful Christmas Day. My new tray purse was in my pocket and I fingered it lovingly, dreaming also of my other presents of which a beautiful new paint box and a baby doll were special ones. But it was lovely to be back in Braid Road. We all loved the house there and the proximity of the Braid Hills. The daughter of the green-keeper at the golf course had become a friend and we often played together. Of course she had to see my new doll. I had always wanted a baby doll with a layette and a shawl. Now, at almost twelve years of age, I had achieved my ambition and my cup of happiness was full except that I was somewhat ashamed to be playing with a doll at my age. Much as I loved Marie and wanted to share her with my friend at the golf course, I covered her up entirely in a blanket when I took her there. But it was Marie that centred in my imaginative play, and I suppose the whole 'thing' of a doll was my imitating my mother and gradually more and more sharing in the caring for my siblings.

This was the period of the phoney war. Everything seemed to go quiet for a while. The full fury of the conflict was yet to come, though never to any great extent in Edinburgh. While great happenings were filling the newspapers and the world held its breath for the next step in the war, our family had its own particular trauma. We had to leave our beloved Braids and go to a house at Bruntsfield, nearer the centre of town. My father was promoted to Office Manager and this house went with the job. While we were proud of Dad's success and happy for him, we were sad to move, especially mother and I. Before doing so in this memoir however I must record two other scenarios of the Braid Road days.

Help for the War Effort

The drawing-room in our house had a large bay window. Poor Mother's lovely room was greatly disturbed when we made the window space into a stage for a concert. Of course I was both producer and principal actress! Jim was stage-manager assisted by Alex, and friends and other cousins were roped in to sing, act and dance. Somewhat to my parents' dismay and amusement, I had invited the whole world and his sister. Amongst others, the entire Brownie pack and its officers from church turned up and neighbours from all round. We had fun trying to accommodate everyone and my parents' hospitality was strained to its limits. But the concert was a great success. It was a happy social occasion in the midst of trying times and it raised quite a good sum of money for the comforts of the troops. For me in addition the creative planning and performing gave great satisfaction.

The money raised was augmented by that from another event, this time at Morag's home. It was a garden fete. Neighbours and friends produced goods for the stalls. Morag's father set up various games and side-shows and her mother provided tea. With adult help Morag and I composed a letter with our donation, to the officer commanding the troops stationed on Inch Keith in the Firth of Forth. We greatly treasured his courteous reply.

Picnic at the Cave

The other scenario is our cave on the hills. Cousin Jim and his circle of friends had arranged a picnic and Ena and I were greatly privileged to be invited. A fire was lit at the entrance to the cave and we cooked sausages on sticks. We relished the special smoky taste, the sausages washed down by lemonade and other soft drinks. The flickering firelight drew us together and the fun and banter of exuberant youth were silenced for a time. As I see it now, looking back, this was a kind of epitaph in advance. Jim and most of the others died in the war. That picnic symbolised the end of an era. For our family, soon to move, this was also so and for me personally it was the time of my leaving the primary school, a significant staging-post.

Chapter 3

Growing Up

Move to Higher Grade

In Scotland there was a qualifying examination which was taken at the age of twelve. The results in this decided the secondary placing of the pupil. For many also it meant a change of school but for us in Gillespie's it meant simply moving up to the Higher Grade. I did strangely badly at this hurdle. All the way until that last year of primary I had been in the top echelon then suddenly things went wrong and I ended up in the C stream. There were five streams, the A and B sections considered to be heading for the university, the Cs for office work and the Ds and Es possibly to be shop-girls or waitresses! From my later life as an educationist I could wax lyrical on the merits and demerits of streaming but I shall avoid the temptation. Suffice it to say that I now found myself amongst the 'middle-of-the-roaders' and away from my former 'buddies', especially Mairi who was placed in the A stream and who was furious on my behalf. I had always been above her in marks before. I was not greatly perturbed apart from the disappointment of not having Mairi in my class, as the full significance had not yet dawned on me. The problem was that only the A and B streams had Latin, a necessity for almost any course at a Scottish university at that time and when, having recovered my motivation and risen once more in my school performance, I acquired an attestation of fitness to go to university at the end of my secondary years thus proving the 'streamers' wrong, I found the lack of Latin a major stumbling block.

My English teacher was willing to coach me had I stayed on to a sixth year which was seen as a pre-university period. Mairi and most of the As and Bs did this. I was now seeing myself as a teacher in primary school and felt that a university degree was not necessary, although in Scotland, unlike England, many teachers in primary schools *were* university graduates. I would leave school and enrol at Moray House Teacher Training College, (now The Faculty of Education in the University of Edinburgh) for a three year course of training, which I subsequently did. It was an important decision for which in the light of my further career I have no regrets and believe was God-guided.

I have often wondered about that 'qualifying' year. What was it that sent me off course? There were probably several factors. War and evacuation with a sudden change of school I shared with many children. The schools had closed temporarily and those children not evacuated were taught in house-groups for a while. Gillespie's and most schools re-opened at the end of 1939.

In addition for me, Alex and I went down with some kind of bug which affected our neck glands and we were off school for some time. Also in that qualifying year I had a teacher I could simply not relate to, and I badly needed an understanding adult at that time. My parents were going through a bad patch in their marriage. I did not comprehend the situation but I was aware that all was not well and it hurt me more than I can say. They were not there so much for me to share my school successes with, or so it seemed to me so my motivation dropped. Although things were never quite the same as they had been in my early years, we all learned to adjust and the family curve of relationships took an upward turn again. Fortunately my wonderful friend Mairi remained closer than ever even if we were in different classes, and a special bonus was that I made new friends in this class, some of whom went on to Moray House with me and whose friendship I have valued into old age. I was happy in my C stream.

Our New Home

The house at number 1, Merchiston Park stood on a corner, four-square to the winds. It was surrounded by a large garden shaded by twenty-two horsechestnut trees. There were outhouses and a garage and, most entrancing of all, there was a well a hundred and eighty feet deep with a channel running from it to the brewery in Fountainbridge. The rooms were large and spacious, three public and several bedrooms including one for the maid! There was an elegant sweeping staircase rising out of a tiled hallway. And there was a green baize door to cut off the kitchen quarters and maid's accommodation from the rest of the house. I suppose it was a typical 19th century dwelling for those accustomed to gracious living. We had come a long way from the flat in Springvalley Gardens. But we were not in fact strangers to this establishment, at least not to the garden. When I was a little girl and we were still in the flat, the then office manager had allowed my mother to sit there. Once again my memory is of Mother reading and me playing and dreaming. This time the environment is a garden, fragrant with the pungent scent of phlox and of wonderful peace except for the hum of insects. My dream-world even had the stimulation of a real castle. This was the well-house, a solid square building with a castellated edge to its roof. I loved it until the day my ball went on that roof and my play ended in tears. Mother had to buy me a new one on our walk home. Little did either of us know, (or did Mother have a dream?) that in a few years' time, this garden and house would be our home.

But 1940 was a difficult time to be moving into this challenging situation. Wartime conditions put paid to any ideas we might have had of playing 'lord of the manor'. There were no servants, and fuel for heating the many rooms was at a premium. Occasionally we did manage to have a fire in what we called the sitting-room, probably the morning-room of former days. And here we eventually brought the piano which needed to be rescued from the freezing drawingroom, and so we could entertain and have our musical evenings, of which more later. But most of the time we lived in the small kitchen where a fire was kept going and only banked down at night. I can still see the two special pails of 'clinker' which were kept topped up for this purpose and which I learned to operate. The fire was in what was for those days a very modern range. It was called, 'All-U-Want' I remember, and turned out to be very little we wanted as it was extremely hard to keep going.

It was a cramped but cosy existence, virtually a working-class, kitchen culture within the surroundings of the middle-class of a different age. I did not understand all this at the time but I realise now how hard it must have been for my parents. They had to furnish and care for the wider 'shell' as it were while we lived in the 'kernel', one particularly onerous task being to provide blackout materials for the numerous windows which had also to be treated for protection against bomb blast. I can remember that Gran, with her practical bent, was a tower of strength and support. She helped my parents for instance to acquire, mainly from auctions, some excellent second hand furnishings. The curtains and pelmets alone for the large windows were a financial liability.

And so, new home, new school regime and new 'state of the world' – all went on apace for me – and in that order. I was laconic in my consideration of world events as an early diary reveals. Perhaps all children were unless they were in the thick of the bombing. We simply went on with our lives. We had a blast shelter. This was the well-house with roof sand-bagged, windows blocked up and an extra metal door added. Inside there was a power point and a kettle and on the dresser in the kitchen was a suitcase with supplies always ready along with toys and books and other diversions, the family ration books and other papers. We each looked after our own gasmask which we carried at all times except baby Joan whose enveloping Mickey Mouse variety had to be carried for her. Our shelter in fact was never used even on the worst night of the Clyde bombing when the raid went on till dawn and Gran stayed over with us. Edinburgh and the east of Scotland generally were mercifully spared apart from a few strikes on the Forth shipping and some bombs shed by aircraft fleeing back to Germany from the Clyde.

Other Wartime Memories

I am constantly amazed at how easily human beings can adapt to circumstances. We got used to clutching a bunch of ration books when we 'did the messages and to accepting the somewhat meagre portions of everything as the sinking of our food convoys had more and more effect. I regret to confess however that my love of butter did lead me personally into evil ways. My mother had tried in vain to stop me over-indulging from the common butter-dish, and eventually resorted to giving us each our own dish. It is the only time in my life that I have consciously stolen anything. I would find ways of taking a little bit from each of the other dishes! We became used to powdered potato and egg and other substitutes for this and that but we (the children) never knew the joy of buying sweets. I had *just* known that experience. Now we left it to Dad.

He used to hide his week's purchase, often amongst the papers in his bureau. The adrenalin pumped when we saw him approach the desk. New clothes could be a problem, involving much careful planning, the functional taking precedence over the pretty or fashionable. Ladies ceased to wear stockings and painted their legs instead even to the seam at the back.

My father, being past the age of call-up, was in a branch of 'Dad's Army'. He was a fire-fighter and roof-spotter based at a house further down Merchiston Park. When the siren wailed he would go off suitably clothed and equipped. We all had to learn to work the stirrup-pump and each household had one. Most homes also had a shelter of some kind or easy access to the public shelters which were strategically placed and well indicated. At school we had frequent shelter and gas-mask drill. This was part of the 'national curriculum' and I take my hat off to the teachers who managed to make these fun activities.

My own contribution at this time was as a Girl Guide. I worked for my National Service badge which involved ninety six hours of serving the community in one way or another. The badge could accrue bars as more sets of ninety six hours were worked and I managed to acquire a few of these. I worked in a woman's hospital taking the flowers out at night and dealing with some of the not so pleasant things in the sluice room. I worked for the ladies in green, The Women's Voluntary Service, filing and running errands. I served on the mobile canteen at Leith Docks. But the job I remember best was my work in the canteen at Waterloo Place, just east of Princes Street. This was more permanent and regular, always on a Sunday night. How I loved the banter and camaraderie of the troops and the fun of working as part of a team! How well I remember coming out after my shift was over into the blackout, with hooded torch, and waiting for my tramcar home. I was fourteen and perfectly safe. Do we need wars to eliminate the horrors of peace?! A year or two later when I had moved up from Guides to Rangers, I became a messenger with a special armband. My parents had to sign their agreement. I used to listen to a radio programme which told the stories of other young people doing brave things in air-raids and I was prepared but this particular service was not needed in Edinburgh.

My Secondary School Years

In many ways this kind of existence hastened my growing up. It seemed to give me a greater sense of purpose and responsibility. I also learned to appreciate what I had, as so much was difficult to acquire. Life went on remarkably smoothly. At school two new friends came to the fore in particular, Frances and Mary. Frances sat beside me in class much of the time. We were very close for about three years and then we drifted apart. My friendship with Mary was to last for the rest of my life. She was a pal at both school and church. In particular she was and still is a very competent pianist and used to accompany me in the heyday of my singing. Mary became a family friend and often played for our musical evenings at home. My father and uncles, Willie Garvie and Dave, all had fine voices. My mother was a pianist and my sisters became so. I too had piano lessons for a time but started too late and never became a sight-reader. I preferred to play by ear. Alex was to become an excellent violinist, playing in school and later university orchestras. And I just loved singing. Dad and I sang duets. I remember one especially which I sang with great enthusiasm at nineteen. It was called, 'Life's Dream is o'er'! My friend Mary was at the centre of all this musical activity. She and Alex loved to play Scottish dance music together. We had wonderful evenings. There was no need for television.

At the door of the Merchiston Park house. Edie, 14, with Joan and Alex.

Throughout my secondary school years I was a part-time foster mother and housewife as I helped my mother in innumerable ways. The entries in my diary make boring reading! I repeatedly 'stir the porridge, wash the dishes, hear homework, put children to bed'. And in and around all this I was working for the Higher Leaving Certificate which was so important. As I stirred the porridge for half an hour each morning, I held a book in my other hand. Early morning was always a good learning time for me. This period of my life too saw Alex forging ahead in *his* school. On return from evacuation he had become a pupil at George Watson's College for Boys, a Merchant Company foundation and fee-paying. He was to become one of its most distinguished students. Joan started at Gillespie's and Dorothy, my last sibling, was born in the summer of 1943. I remember that my father met me at the station as I returned from a school berry-picking camp, with the news that I had a new sister. Somehow I had expected a boy and had to get used to the notion of having another sister but I soon took her to my heart and because of the age-difference, fifteen and a half years, became almost a third parent.

The year before this Auntie Jean and Uncle Willy had had a son, Graham, their first child after ten years of marriage. This must have been a great joy. Jim was in the airforce and Ena was working as a telephonist in the Post Office. They had both come successfully through secondary school. Anne was in Kelso High School and Doris and Norma attended Alva Academy in Clackmannanshire. The family had been evacuated to that area and stayed on after the war. Uncle Billy was in the army.

So we all progressed but in 1944 came the great sadness. I quote from my diary,

> 'It is with a heavy heart [that] I have to record the death on active service of my cousin Jim. He was killed on the morning of 22nd December while returning from a bombing sortie over Germany. He was only twenty years of age and was about to become engaged to Joyce M'Donald, a girl that he had known for about four or five years. His body was brought up from England where the accident occurred and buried in Liberton cemetery.'

I was devastated and felt that I had lost a brother. Ena was never the same again. She and Jim had been very close, and not only in age. About the same time Jim's friend Pete was also killed. As a family we always believed that Ena and Pete had been special friends. Ena never married and became a strange, very private person for the rest of her life. It was this kind of family grief we shared with so many in this terrible war.

The Concert Circuit

My love of the stage and of performing had never waned and continued throughout the war years. As a primary school pupil I had joined the dancing class after school. Now in my secondary years I became a pupil of Ella Allan, the family friend with the Dramatic Society who was also a teacher of elocution. I embarked on a course which eventually led to my gaining the LLCM (Licentiate of the London College of Music and Dramatic Art) with teaching diploma. I began to take part now as a regular in her productions. But, best of all were the one-off concerts in and around Edinburgh. There were a number of people in a pool of performers, singers and musicians of various kinds, dancers and elocutionists. They formed concert parties when called upon and performed in old people's homes, hospitals and town halls. My elocution teacher was one of this group and sometimes she would ask me or another of her pupils to stand in for her. I became an elocutionist. I also sang in some of the concerts as my soprano voice had developed since the Kelso days and I was in the special choir at school.

Uncle Willie Garvie had a particular interest in all this and encouraged me to take part in other concerts which he organised for the old people in Portobello and Musselburgh. He was in touch with these groups through his welfare work with the police. I even found myself replying to the Toast to the Lassies at Burns' Suppers where I also sang and recited the works of our Scottish bard. I have Uncle Willie to thank for a growing and lasting love for Scottish poetry and song, later to be enhanced at Moray House. The Portobello days leave warm memories. In their home at Straiton Place Auntie Jean and Uncle Willie were genial hosts.

One event of the concert circuit stands out in my memory. We were performing in Saughton Prison. The 'captive' audience was one of the most appreciative that I have ever faced. I gave them Scots comedy and they loved it. Afterwards the wardresses as the women officers were then called, gave us a wonderful supper which greatly appealed to my sixteen-year-old appetite. But I still chuckle when I recall a conversation with the singer as we were approaching the prison through a series of clanging gates. He informed me with a serious face that he would sing 'Bless this House', a song I knew. I also sang it. In my naivety I believed him at first and was struck with horror when I thought of some of the lines …

> …*Bless these walls so firm and stout,*
> *keeping want and trouble out.*
> *Bless the people here within,*
> *Keep them pure and free from sin.*
> *Bless this door that it may prove*
> *ever open to joy and love.*

Needless to say my friend was not serious and all was well. I could breathe again.

Deepening Awareness of God

Unlike many young people on the edge of adulthood I did not leave church and churchy things as an aspect of the childhood I had grown out of. The church services, Sunday-school and then Bible Class, were an integral part pf my life and meant a great deal to me. I became an enthusiastic Sunday-school teacher. I also joined something called The Girls' Association where I met one of its national officers at a Bible School. This was Irene Glass who became another lifelong friend. She trained as a Church of Scotland missionary and later served in India for thirty-five years. My discussions with her and the whole ambience of my church life at that time had a profound effect. I considered the mission field as a possible future for myself just as I saw myself in the theatre! Were these two incompatible? I was not to become a missionary of the church, nor was I to go on the stage professionally. My parents, guided by the headmistress and my teachers, encouraged me towards a teaching career and so it was to be. Nevertheless I did feel some kind of calling and the power and guidance of God became very real.

Another contributory factor to this was my debut with something called, at that time, the University Women's Camps for Schoolgirls, to which I was introduced by one of my teachers. It later became the Student Christian Movement in Schools. These summer 'camps', usually in a building of some kind and not under canvas, were held all over

Britain. As a schoolgirl I attended the one at Lochearnhead in 1942 and Morebattle near Kelso in 1944.Later I became an officer, first in a junior capacity responsible for the 'fun and games' and finally as Chaplain or Camp Leader. It was a Christian foundation and we had regular prayer-time and Bible Study. Also I was introduced to other ways of Christian worship. For instance prayers were sometimes read from a book and sometimes chanted. My religious horizons were considerably expanded, a further extension of that experience all those years ago in Glasgow when I realised that teddy-bears could be of different colours!

The 'Extra-curricular'

By this I mean those things which did not come into the on-going strands of my life. The doings and events of home, school and church and even my stage activities formed the core of my life in those secondary school years, but there was a growing 'other' which really took off at this time and became almost a constant in itself. It was two-pronged, the first being my love of reading and the second of travel. My mother had loved reading as a girl though she found little time for it as a busy housewife and my father had always aspired to go beyond the immediate boundaries. He nearly went to the far east as a tea-planter at one stage. The war cramped my style for a while but, helped by the Scottish Youth Hostels Association and by the acquisition of a bicycle I was able to go out and about quite considerably even at that time. Through my rambles with Mairi and other friends and later Alex and his pals, I became better acquainted with the environs of Edinburgh and beyond and to learn of the lovely country of Scotland which was my heritage.

For Alex and me, the Pentland Hills had replaced the Braids as our regular playground. It was Dad who first introduced us to them. He took us walking there when we were quite small. We loved especially the walk from Balerno to Flotterstone over a pass in these hills. It was about seven miles and the 'prize' at the end of the tramp was a glorious bacon and egg tea which we reckoned we could smell long before we saw the cottage where two elderly ladies ran a tearoom. We even managed during these war years to keep up the annual family holiday. We went to Belhaven near Dunbar which was much nearer home than Largs or Nairn. No-one at that time wanted to go too far from home-ground. At

Hostelling, 1945

Belhaven we stayed in The Manor House, a guest-house owned by an eccentric minister's widow and run by her house-keeper, an ex-nurse who was also a spiritualist medium. It was a strange, old-fashioned establishment. We all sat down to meals together presided over by Mrs Burnett in her Edwardian dress, wig, and large hat which she wore inside and out. Old Nan, the table-maid, was also a relic of the past in her aprons, cuffs and caps. Afternoon tea on the lawn, my father roped in to carry the urn, and strange goings-on behind the drawn blinds of the nurse's room, are vivid memories.

I could write a whole chapter on this fascinating place including memories of the old-fashioned plumbing and lighting, the tower whose bedroom was supposed to be haunted and which I slept in once or twice, enjoying frissons of terror as I imagined all kinds of strange sounds, and the roof which could be walked on where Dad and I watched a spitfire dogfight on an exciting night of air-raid alarm before joining the rest of the household in the cellar shelter. I remember giggling naughtily at the elderly guests in their nightcaps and minus teeth. The candle-carrying brigade dispersing to their rooms on the all-clear must have frightened the ghosts rather than the other way round!

A taste of the exotic? I can see now that my growing interest in new places and faces and my love of travel stemmed from many seeds. At that time my physical travel was limited. Perhaps this was a good thing. I needed to know my own place, to know myself, before launching further afield, but my reading took me far and wide.

A Bridging Experience

It was this in more ways than one. I refer to my short spell as a 'Utility Landgirl' during the summer of 1945. First it carried me over from school to college and second from local adventure to pastures new, no pun intended. The regular Land Army had been one of the women's services right through the war, replacing male farm-workers who had been called up. At harvest time, extra hands were required and students were useful recruits. This additional force was known affectionately or otherwise as the Utility Land Army.

My leaving school in 1945 coincided more or less with the end of the war. Victory in Europe or V.E.Day was on the 8th of May and Victory in Japan or V.J.Day was on the 15th of August. I left Gillespie's at the end of June. For the world and for me personally a chapter had closed. It was a time of new beginnings. In the autumn I would start my training as a primary teacher. For now I would engage in this bit of service for the community and enjoy myself at the same time. I had got used to this during the war. My Girl Guide National Service commitment was, I think, another important seed in my life. From then on I felt the need to give service of one kind or another, sometimes within my 'curriculum' and sometimes outside it. It took many forms, depending upon my awareness of need and of my own capacity to help. And always I learned a lot and enjoyed the experience.

As I did this one. The first 'posting' I shared with Mairi. We worked on a farm near Dalbeattie in the Borders. The farmer was a genial man weighing over twenty stone who seemed surprised when the seat of the binder dropped considerably as he sat on it! For all his bulk he was nimble on his feet and was all over the place keeping an eagle eye on his workers. We were kept hard at it, stooking in the fields stacking in the yard and then threshing. There was no combine harvester in those days. Occasionally there were other jobs such as hoeing the plants grown for cattle-feed. I learned so much and a new vocabulary to go with it, some of it very rich indeed!

This was a new world for me and a different culture. I loved it and I enjoyed working in the open air. I developed a special affection for the beautiful Clydesdale horses, the gentle giants of pre-tractor days, though at the same time I had a healthy respect for their large hooves and teeth. As a townie I was feeling my way. We were there for several weeks then Mairi had to return for her sixth year of secondary school. I had a new assignment, this time in the north of the country at Fearn in Rosshire. The harvest was just that bit later here. The work was much the same except that the tractor had arrived. Also the whole operation was bigger and less personal, supervised by a foreman or grieve. I joined a whole group of girls and we were housed in army huts (in the Borders Mairi and I had been in the village hall along with others working on different farms). In the north we were conscious of being part of a large force of 'troops' as we were near both naval and airforce bases and a prisoner of war camp. There was constant troop movement and activity especially at the time of the Battle of Britain commemoration. Needless to say we girls had a wonderful time in our off-duty hours. I acquired a Welsh RAF boyfriend with whom I fell passionately in love! I used to sing in the fields as I worked and one day I was attempting an aria from 'One Fine Day' only the first part of which I could manage in Italian. I was suddenly startled to hear a fine male voice from the other end of the field singing along with me in faultless Italian. We had been joined by prisoners of war and we worked and sang together. So much for enemies! And so to another new world for me, that of student days at Moray House Teacher Training College in the Royal Mile of Edinburgh.

Chapter 4

Training as a Primary Teacher

Historic Moray House

The training college, set in one of Edinburgh's most interesting and historic areas, was an education in itself. The Canongate in the lower part of the Royal Mile is steeped in Edinburgh's past. Moray House, like Huntly House and Milton House and others, recalls the great families of another age. They still exist in name at least and some have the old building or part of it still in place. There is, for instance, the famous balcony at Moray House where Argyll watched his enemy Montrose going past on his way to the gallows, not realising that he himself would shortly be taking the same road. The Canongate on a dark winter's afternoon could be almost spooky at times as I left college and made my way to a bus-stop for home, passing closes and wynds (open-ended passages) which were reminders of many a grisly deed. Edinburgh's old town is on a ridge which runs from the castle at the top to Holyrood Abbey and Palace at the foot. At one time, where Princes Street Gardens now lie, was the Nor' Loch, a murky stretch of water and natural defence. The wynds had easy access to it and who knows what or who ended there?! My lively imagination was constantly stimulated and especially as during my college years I became particularly interested in the music of the past and in the Edinburgh of Burns' time when the city seethed with litterati. I was privileged to have my education as a teacher amid such richness!

Study and Play

My headmistress had been right. Teaching was definitely for me but I did have to learn that living children were not quite so amenable as those bedposts I used to teach in my imaginative play! They were breathing, lively people and the classroom became a community whose agenda was the responsibility of the teacher. I enjoyed the challenge. The practice teaching in a number of different schools in the city was the favourite part of my training but I also enjoyed the studies. I believe that the course was a good one, comprehensive of so much in both theory and practice. The three years to 1948 seemed to pass incredibly quickly.

They were also greatly enriched by the opportunities they gave for 'performing'. I joined the operatic society. Our music lecturer, Tom McCourt, had a special interest in 18th century ballad opera and other genres of that time. We staged a number of operas, one of which, 'The Highland Fair', was part of the Fringe in the Edinburgh Festival one year. This was the nearest I had come so far to being 'on the stage' professionally. We were performing in the Gateway, an old-fashioned theatre in Leith Walk. It had a traditional spiral staircase down which we all ran to the summons of 'Beginners ready please'. I defy anyone, amateur or professional, not to feel those butterflies when this call comes. The adrenalin begins to flow.

But in addition to theatre work I was privileged to go sometimes with Dr McCourt when he was giving a lecture outside college. He would call upon me to demonstrate for him. On one memorable occasion the lecture took the form of a musical soirée. It was held in the famous Gladstone's Land, now cared for by the National Trust for Scotland, and situated in the Lawnmarket at the top end of the Royal Mile. This was just the right setting for the music. I can see the room now, the grand piano amongst the period furniture, and the light from the blazing log fire dancing on its polished surfaces. Dr McCourt, his pianist, myself and the members of the selective audience were all in evening dress. I can feel once again the attentive atmosphere of concentrated enjoyment. I was given a slot of my own at this concert and, on being asked for an encore, I sang 'The Road to the Isles', in honour of its writer Kenneth Macleod who was one of the audience. The quiet but sincere approval of this elderly gentleman with the long white beard was something I greatly valued.

Church Leading Soprano

For a short time I was leading soprano at Morningside Parish Church when the College Church organist left to go there and asked me to accompany him. This happened during my college years and gave a whole new dimension to my singing. I enjoyed some of the loveliest church anthems and oratorios, and with much trepidation at first tackled the solo parts. I even rose to those in the Messiah at one stage. My father was a tremendous help and encouraged me to ever greater heights in more ways than one. He would sit in the congregation beating time and criticising my efforts in love.

My period with the Morningside Parish choir had its comic side too. The 'uniform' consisted of a gown and mortarboard complete with tassel. To the disgust of our leading alto who was a longstanding choir member and a bit of a tartar I kept getting my mortarboard on at a crooked angle and invariably the tassel was over the wrong eye! Then there was the problem of the 'lead-in', first in the Session House where we lined up before entering to the singing of 'Oh enter then His gates with praise' from Psalm 100, and second during or at the start of an anthem when a solo brought in the rest of the choir. The Session House had its own piano and it was necessary for me to strike the right note on it and hold this in my head while we lined up, then lead us all in the verse. It had to be compatible with the voluntary being played by the organist as he was still playing when we started and the people could hear us. This was a nightmare for me. Often through sheer panic the note would go astray with disastrous results and red faces all round as we marched into church. Another problem was knowing exactly where to come in when the introduction to an anthem demanded very careful sight-reading and timing. I had much to learn in this department. On one occasion the introduction had been played four times before I was galvanised into action by a poke in the back from the choir member behind! But what a wonderful educative experience it was! It also seemed to enhance, through my enjoyment of the music, my growing awareness of God's presence in my life. I joined the Youth Fellowship in this church and again I taught in Sunday-school. There was a time indeed when I seemed to spend most of my week at Church.

Home Memories and the Tripe Story

I must have been one of the few teacher trainees with a baby sister, very useful for my child development studies. I still helped a lot at home. By this time Joan was well into primary school and Alex in the secondary department of Watson's. At one stage I did a teaching practice in the class he had just left, the top junior. I remember he and his friends

The Family, 1948

teasing me about my blackboard work when they peeped in at lunchtime. But a home memory of these years which stands out for me is the 'adventure' of the tripe.

Mother and Dad had gone on holiday and I was in charge. We had a young German visitor, Margarethe, at the time. Meat was still rationed as were most commodities. It was the custom of our butcher to send, by delivery boy, just what he had. There was no question of ordering what you wanted. One morning I was dismayed to find that the butcher's parcel contained a soggy lump of tripe. I had never cooked this in my life though Mother had given it to us and I had quite enjoyed it cooked with onion in milk. It looked now somewhat grey and shrivelled, a bit like someone's grubby knitting, and it smelt horrible. The family dared me to give it to them with dire threats. What to do?

I had a little meat or mince left over so I postponed the evil moment by putting the tripe in a saucepan of water and laying it aside on the cooker. But the next day something would have to be done. The kitchen smelt of tripe. I put the saucepan in the garden for a while! 'How do you cook tripe?', I asked our German guest. 'Tripe? Vhat eez zese tripe?' asked Margarethe, gazing into the offending pan. She eventually came up with an elaborate recipe which I could not follow, containing ingredients which it was not possible to obtain in any case. Then, at my look of desperation, she solved the problem by suggesting with a laugh that I 'meens it down, put it in a pie so ze family don't know vhat zey eat'!

So I did, first softening the tripe by hours of cooking on the kitchen range. I did find an onion and I used a lump of margarine. Then, well after everyone was in bed, I spent an hour with Mother's ancient mincer and filled two pyrex dishes with the ground tripe. Next day I boiled potatoes, covered the tripe with these and put the dishes in the oven. To my delight and relief the result was appetising. Alex came in from school and gobbled his meal without question while he read a book as always and the younger ones also ate with no queries. Margarethe and I exchanged conspiratorial smiles and then I confessed. There was a big laugh all round. I remember writing of this incident to my parents in their highland hotel. I received a postcard in return full of the joys of Inverness but spoilt by the effect of a strange odour following them. They thought it might be tripe!

A Teaching Practice Adventure

Another strong memory of these college years comes from the teaching practice I did in Alva Academy where my cousins Doris and Norma were at school. We were supposed to do some teaching during the long college vacation and I had wangled this one so that I could visit friends and relatives in Clackmannanshire at the same time. I couldn't stay with Auntie Gladys as there was no room but we had family friends in a place called Sauchie, near Alloa, easy to get to from Alva. Norma was in the top class of the junior school and this is where I did my teaching. It was fun. We both enjoyed it.

One weekend I had gone home to Edinburgh. The bus to Stirling broke down and by the time it had recovered and we finally reached Stirling where I had to change, I had missed the last bus to Sauchie. I had not enough money to stay in a hotel and it was getting late to go hunting for digs. Nothing daunted I went to the police in their headquarters near Stirling castle. A burly policeman with a large torch took me up a stair in a seedy tenement close by. It was not the most salubrious of areas but presumably the police knew the 'safe houses'.

The policeman banged on a door. 'Can ye gie this lassie a bed for the night?', he enquired of the man who opened to us. 'Na, we're full up' was the ungracious response. We climbed another flight. This time the reply was, 'Aye, bring her in. We've got anither ane in here'. I met the 'ither ane' in the kitchen/livingroom where we were given a good supper and shown to our room. We shared a double bed!

To my unpractised ear 'the ither ane' had an English, possibly London, accent but she assured me she was Polish and had been working in a camp for Polish officers near North Berwick, a seaside town in East Lothian. She was going on to Glasgow for some reason in the morning. But what did intrigue me were the contents of her suitcase. It was full of chocolate bars and other difficult to get sweets, also soap and various toiletries. I said nothing, got myself to the edge of the bed, fully clothed, and was soon asleep with the healthy weariness of youth.

We were wakened in the morning by the landlady throwing open the door and calling to 'the ither ane' to get up. Her bus left before mine. There had to be a disciplined ordering for washing which was accomplished at the kitchen sink. There was no bathroom. The man of the house had just left for work so the way was now clear. While the 'ither ane' had breakfast, I washed, and then had mine. It was an excellent meal too. For this Bed, Evening Meal and Breakfast I paid five shillings. I then went off for my bus to Alva and my day's teaching. Somehow I must have informed my Sauchie friends of what had happened. Perhaps the police helped. It was quite an adventure though I had rather fancied a night in the cells!

The story had an interesting sequel. Later that summer and just before Mairi and I returned to university and college respectively, we were in North Berwick, working on a student placement at a Dr Barnardo's children's home.

In the course of conversation with staff the story of my night in Stirling was related. I had remembered the girl's very un-Polish name and when I mentioned it here there was a sense of shock in the air. The 'ither ane' had been one of their girls who had kept running away. The police had often found her at the camp for Polish officers and had brought her back. The organisation was pledged to look after girls until they were eighteen. The lass had been seventeen and they were concerned about her. She had really disappeared this time and my sleeping with her and learning that she was heading for Glasgow was a new lead. But in a few months anything could have happened. I have often wondered how the story ended. But no doubt for a start-off she had done a brisk business with her case of purloined goods!

Hostelling

Before bringing the story of my college years to an end and heading for the next staging-post, I want to tell of three further adventures of that time. The first is a hostelling holiday in 1946 with my cousin Ena. How I ever managed to persuade her to accompany me I cannot recall. She was not one for adventures of this kind, but persuade her I did and we set off for Callander and Loch Vennacher in central Scotland.

Our first hostel was Craig Dhu near Callander. I have no recollection of how we got that far but I do remember the second day. We hoped to be at Inverbeg Hostel on the other side of Loch Lomond by late afternoon or early evening and we finally did so by a mixture of walking and sailing. A steamer took us from Trossachs to Stronachlachar. We had a wet and windy sail on the choppy waters of Loch Katrine in one of the oldest boats of its kind and still in operation I believe. The hills came to meet the loch, their lower slopes clothed with trees. Here and there a small dwelling would appear, the tiny chimney giving smoky evidence of a lonely existence within.

Arriving in Stronachlachar, we took to the road, making for Loch Lomond and a ferry that would take us across. For the most part we had Loch Arklet on our left and hilly moorland on our right except towards the end when the moor gave way to a number of small houses straggling up a hillside near the place where a stream enters Loch Lomond in a series of roaring falls. Just a little further we would board the ferry. We waited a long time for it and were alarmed by the stormy aspect of the loch, and more alarmed still when the ferry arrived, as there was something wrong with the engine! The rain poured down while we waited, not at all relishing what was bound to be an uncomfortable and somewhat hazardous crossing.

During our wait we saw a young man and a girl, busy with a small canoe. They seemed to be preparing to launch it, having put up three sails and donned oilskins. It looked to us like suicide, setting out on the turbulent waters in that frail little craft. But after we were installed in our own boat which was not all that larger, we saw that the canoe was racing southwards with the wind in its sails and seemingly weathering the billows. Although I thought several times that our boat might capsize, we did at last reach the other side safely with the gloomy old boatman telling us that it was 'a guid nine mile tae Inverbeg' and predicting that we would be unlikely to find a lift. As if to spite him, however, a lorry came along just as we scrambled up to the road and we were soon spinning along to our destination.

We had been squeezed into the cabin beside the driver and another man who had thumbed a lift. It was uncomfortable but fun. I teased the men by spinning yarns about what I did for a living. I started as a milliner and ended in a biscuit factory! We finally arrived at the Inverbeg hostel, another timber building about a hundred yards from the road at the head of Glen Douglas and directly opposite the all-famous Ben Lomond.

There was a strange kilted, bare-footed warden at this place who had a 'thing' about the shaking and folding of blankets. The next day we had a long walk by the loch in pouring rain particularly heavy on the stretch from Luss to Balloch. The hostel there had been someone's stately home and was a large, castle-like building very different from the wooden structure we had become accustomed to. The cooking utensils were at a premium here I remember. I also recall Ena putting on an apron and cleaning her shoes after our ten-mile walk in the pouring rain when all I wanted to do was collapse in a heap! There is no accounting for folks. But the holiday had been 'time out', worthwhile for both of us and a learning experience in so many ways. My thanks to the Scottish Youth Hostels Association.

In 1947 I went hostelling again, this time with college friends Leslie, Kathleen and Betty. We went to the Isle of Arran in the west of Scotland. Leslie and I cycled round the island and the other two walked or bussed. It is a pretty place, offering many beauties of land and sea with the hill of Goatfell rising above Brodick the main town. There is a good road all round and two main arteries across the centre, the String and the Ross. We were on all of these roads. We also stayed in all the hostels, four at that time, placed at strategic points.

My main memory of this holiday was of the intense heat. The whole country experienced this and it went on for a long time. It also gave rise to the polio epidemic. A great many people were ill, especially children. It was well into September before the heat eased and Scotland at least returned to its 'usual' weather. I remember that one day in Aran all we could do was to don bathing suits and lie in a burn. The outside tap at Brodick Hostel failed just as I had discovered my marmalade turned upside down in my rucksack! It was a sticky problem but somehow I survived.

Cruise to the Shetlands

We were all so much enjoying the lifting of wartime restrictions on travel. I for one made the most of it. In addition to my walking, cycling and hostelling I reached out even more adventurously later in that same year of 1947 and after the heatwave had broken. I went on a cruise to the Shetland Islands, the ship leaving from Leith. I was nineteen and on my own. The twelve days which involved six nights at sea and six in a hotel on the main Shetland island, cost £16!

I was on the St Magnus, a fair-sized steamer holding close on four hundred passengers. We left Leith at 7.00 in the evening and after a smooth night, came into Aberdeen. I must have slept, for the next thing I remember was a change of the ship's motion and a gradual quietening down of the engine. We were then subject to a series of vibrations and noises which heralded the docking. It was 4.00 am and still quite dark. I rose quickly and went with others to the famous Aberdeen fish-market. All the little fishing smacks were drawn up along the dockside, the fishermen unloading the fish into boxes in lines under the shelter of an enormous shed. Every conceivable type of fish was there, from small insignificant herring to large flat plaice. Auctioneers' notices requesting vendors not to loiter around the stands were hanging at frequent intervals and carts were ready with their owners standing in little groups, waiting for the selling to begin. A general air of bustle and expectancy seemed to fill the shed. We left before an inadvertent movement of an arm could land us with a crate of catfish! There was time before sailing again to explore the Granite City and this we did, and were very impressed with the grandeur of its buildings. By evening we were on our way to Orkney and the sea began to misbehave. The Pentland Firth is famous for its storms. The North Sea and the Atlantic Ocean meet here and don't always agree! I ate my supper but not without some effort of will, and strangely slept well, even through the berthing noises at Kirkwall. After landing here I was able to find Margaret Donald another college friend. This was her home and she and her family were extremely hospitable. Would that I could linger to describe adequately this interesting 'nordic' world I had now reached. It is another world, bare but attractive in its virtually treeless expanse and in many ways more Scandinavian still than Scottish even after five centuries of the change. The Orkney and Shetland Islands belonged to Norway until 1471.

The sea was reasonably calm as we made our way through the northern Orkney islands but as we moved into the open sea we pitched and rolled once more until we came abreast of Fair Isle and in its lee. Here a passenger was met by a small boat manned by lusty islanders which had come from the western side of Fair Isle. There were no facilities for ships at that time. The rest of us watched with awe and trepidation as our fellow passenger judged the appropriate time to jump from ship to small boat! First the luggage went, then the passenger. There was a general sigh of relief when he judged it right!

Leaving Fair Isle behind we resumed our wild progress until the southern projection of Shetland shut us off from the Atlantic and we had only one sea to cope with. We had a night in the port of Lerwick, the principal town of the islands, and then set off next morning by coach for Hillswick on the west side of the main island and our final destination. Returning visitors went back to Lerwick in our buses. We were in a very pleasant hotel, timber built (I'm sure it swayed in the gales), roomy and comfortable. I had a lovely room at the top. But my main memory of my stay is the food. After years of rationing which was still going on I just could not believe the scene of plenty which Shetland presented, especially the abundant butter supply!

Shetland is even more treeless than Orkney, with constant wind and storms sweeping across the bare spaces and scattered community. I had the impression of being all the time on the top of cliffs. In the week I was there I managed to imbibe something of its flavour, the constant boom of the restless sea and the screech of seabirds, many species I had not seen before, the stark rocks and lighthouses, the pure, clear air stinging in its freshness and the peculiar 'colour' of the northern light – all left a deep impression. And this against the cosy comfort of the hotel lounge with its blazing fire. I remember reading Cronin's 'Far from the Madding Crowd', which seemed appropriate as I curled up on a window seat, the curtains drawn against the gale.

A few highlights remain potent memories. There was the auction at Lochend in aid of church funds, followed by a dance. Ten of us from the hotel were packed into cars and taken off into the hinterland. The lengthening evening shadows crept over the sea-lochs and grassy cliff-tops and Shetland ponies ran from us, tossing their manes. Suddenly amid the emptiness there appeared a large, barn-like building, and we joined the surprising number of vehicles parked around it. It seemed as though the scattered community of mainland Shetland had all come together for the occasion.

The hall was filling up fast. It was lit by lamps which had to be pumped up every now and then. For the auction which was the first item on the agenda, we sat on benches. About half way through the proceedings large mugs of tea were passed along and huge wedges of sandwiches. I managed to consume my share in spite of having eaten a substantial dinner in the hotel. I was fascinated by the nature of the items to be auctioned, everything from a silk purse to a ewe lamb.

By midnight the auction was over and the dance began. The fiddlers and accordionists hardly halted between dances which were mainly of the country variety, such as quadrilles and lancers. In the latter my partner was a burly fisherman who virtually lifted me off the ground as the set swung round in an almost rugby-scrum like huddle. By 3.00 am I and the others from the hotel were utterly exhausted. We decided to call it a day, or a night! But the revelry went on till six o'clock I believe. To complete our enjoyment of the event, the Northern Lights flashed and sparkled above us, as we journeyed home. Even the Shetlanders had never seen them so bright. We sang all the way. It had been a memorable occasion, leaving me with an increasing impression of the warmth and friendliness of Shetlanders who knew how to enjoy themselves and to welcome the stranger. Of course I had to buy some knitted goods and I visited homes where the cottage industry was still very much alive. I also visited several light-houses, one being at the end of a cliff walk with steep drops on either side, and the ladder to the light being on the *outside* of the building! Then there was the unforgettable occasion when four of us encountered a school of porpoises when we were in a rowing-boat. The huge fish followed us like an army in formation. I am sure they were simply curious and would not have done us any harm but they could have turned our boat over if they had gone underneath. It was a scary experience from our first sighting of them when the round black object which was the head of one looked for all the world like a mine, very much in our minds only two years after the end of the war.

Our week in Hillswick passed all too quickly and soon the coaches had returned for us, bringing others to take our places. We left Lerwick at 9.00 pm that evening, once again on the St Magnus. There was quite a crowd waving us off. The sea was a little calmer than it had been on our outward journey and we had a pleasant run to Orkney, where the purser had arranged a trip to Scapa Flow, stopping at the Churchill Barrier. It was moving to see this evocative place, so recently a big part of our wartime lives. I said a silent prayer for the souls of so many, both British and enemy, whose place of rest it was. That night I stayed on deck till late. The ship pitched and tossed and caused alarm when the engine suddenly stopped in the middle of the Pentland Firth. It was some comfort to see on our port side, the lights of the St Clement which had left Kirkwall at the same time as ourselves. We eventually started again and made it to Aberdeen, which we crawled out of in thick fog, the horn blowing every five minutes and the harbour bell ringing three peels at intervals as we glided into the North Sea. Only then did I go to my bunk and sleep. When I awoke we were in the Firth of Forth under a clear sky with the island, Inch Keith, coming up fast. Soon we were safely back in the harbour of Leith. It had been twelve days of wonderful new experience, the first holiday I had ventured on my own, but by no means the last. I had discovered the joy of meeting not only new places but new faces, and that I could thrive on such excursions.

The End of my Course

I ended my college career as a runner-up for the Dixon Teaching prize and as a winner of a Currie prize (3rd in the year). This latter honour I had known nothing about until the closing assembly and prize-giving.

I was sitting right at the front in the balcony and had to extricate myself and run down two flights of stairs to enter the hall on the ground floor. I recall that in my confusion – disbelief – delight – I ran to the basement and had to come up again! I was also very conscious as I eventually went forward for my prize that I was dressed ready to take off on a cycling holiday and not for such a formal occasion as this. I lived and relived the mixed emotions of those few minutes in the days ahead with Mairi in the highlands. And while I was away, I learned in a letter from my mother that I had passed highly in the oral section of my LLCM examination. My studies were over (or so I thought) and the world was my oyster.

Chapter 5

First Jobs

Holiday in the Highlands

I have often thought that the young people of today have too much too soon and that at a very early age they have little left to challenge them or to look forward to. One good thing that the war did for me and those of my generation who survived was to restrict our options in such a way that we learned later to appreciate what life really had to offer. Instead of rushing off at the age of twenty to do a 'gap' year in Australia or somewhere far away I began travelling in a gradually opening Scotland and came to know more about my own lovely country. The Shetland trip had been a wonderful eye-opener but I have to thank in particular the Scottish Youth Hostels Association (SYHA) for the start and gradual development of my 'release' into a wider world. Before I return to the 'curricular' of my life as it were, I must speak of a special hostelling holiday which took me to some of the loveliest parts of Scotland and which acted as a divider between college and my first teaching job just as the farm work had done between school and college.

Mairi and I had three weeks of glorious freedom. We set off first of all for Glen Clova in Perthshire where there was a hostel giving access to the famous Lochnagar, a mountain in spite of its name though there is also a small loch of the name. We were accompanied on the first part of our trip by Helen, Mairi's older sister. Our bicycles, by today's standards, left much to be desired. Mine had no gears at all and I found myself walking rather than cycling even on some of the downward slopes, the hills so steep and my free-wheel so free that it was dangerous to do otherwise. My luggage was carried in old army haversacks purchased at an army and navy store and tied on either side of my seat by pieces of string! Talk about going out in faith! We aimed to see the sunrise from the top of Lochnagar so it was a night climb from Glen Clova. We cycled as far as possible and then left our bicycles trustingly in the heather and proceeded on foot. There was quite a large number of people converging on the mountain that night from three different starting points. I had spotted the plan in the 'Sunday Post'. It had seemed a novel way to start our holiday. So here we were plodding steadily upwards in the wake of a party we should have met with earlier but we had misjudged the distance and so were late. Now we kept arriving at the resting-points just as the party was moving on. But we never got lost as the skirl of the bagpipes was carried back to us on the midsummer breeze.

A treacherous mist defeated our efforts to reach the summit and we had to be content with having reached a level where we could enjoy an amazing sunrise. We stood in reverent silence as the vast golden orb exploded over the horizon and the shadows around us took on the firmness of reality. 'Does this happen every morning?', I asked myself, and I had perhaps my first sense of the permanent in the ephemeral, though I could not then have expressed it.

Helen left us soon after this event as she had to be back at work and Mairi and I made our way across the central highlands to the west including the Isle of Skye. The roads, many of which had never been tarmacked, and were now in an extremely poor state through neglect in the war years, did not offer the best conditions for cycling. Add to this that it rained heavily every day and that the hostels in this part were somewhat primitive with drying facilities at a premium, and you could be forgiven for thinking that here was a recipe for disaster. Strangely it was not. We were young, full of energy and ripe for challenge. A few particular memories leap into sight and bring back a glow of warmth and pleasure.

Our arrival in Skye is one of these. We had had a stormy crossing from Kyle of Lochalsh to Portree and the boat was very late. The others making for Staffin hostel went on the bus which had waited for the boat. Mairi and I were the only two cyclists. Our fellow hostellers waved us off, promising to let the warden know we were on our way in case he locked us out. It was as well they did. It took us four hours to go quite a short distance and our arrival was long past 11.00 pm, the official time of 'lights out'.

The rain poured down as we left Portree and made for the north-east. We had to cycle in the teeth of a howling gale. Every so often it was necessary to dismount and lift the bicycles over rock, strewn across the road. To our left the Old Man of Storr, a well-known Skye hill, loomed out of the swirling mist and a creaking boathouse door on the right sent shivers down my spine. All the stories of the haunted moorland gained credence at this moment. Would we ever arrive at the hostel? Occasionally the scent of peat smoke wafted towards us, and then over a rise would appear in the gloom the lamplight from a cottage. At last there was the familiar triangle with SYHA on it. What a relief! And how wonderful to be greeted in the yard by the understanding warden with his soft Gaelic English. He urged us to be quiet as everyone was in bed. But they had made up sandwiches for us, a luxury indeed. The warden held a torch while we unhitched our gear and entered the welcome warmth. Food never tasted so good. An extra bonus for me was a parcel from home with several more goodies and of course a letter.

The hostel camaraderie was a constant as we pursued our way round Skye, up the west coast of mainland Scotland and then over to the east. We were able to enjoy some spectacular scenery and we met so many interesting and lovely people. To match our sunrise experience at Lochnagar we had a special sunset one, when we were at Carn Dearg hostel in the north west. The rain had ceased, as it often did in the evening, and the world burst into triumphant colour for which no descriptive words can do justice. The warden called us all outside to witness it. There we stood, a group of normally boisterous young people, in silent awe at God's gift in the western sky. The war was not far behind and somehow this splendour had something of the effect upon the Israelites of old when they saw God's bow in the sky. It was uplifting and full of hope.

The chain on Mairi's bike broke when we were in the Shieldaig and Torridon area. We did some hard walking to the nearest rail-station. Mairi went south and home and I went further north in Caithness to the croft home of yet another college friend, Dora Stewart. I was fascinated by the work here and especially that of the sheepdogs. Dora's mother had gone blind when her son was killed in the war. I was terrified but full of admiration as she managed to cook on the open peat-fire. My stay in this place was so comfortable after the privations of the hostels. I enjoyed the bannocks spread thickly with butter and crowdie (cottage cheese) and I loved going up the wooden steps from the stone-flagged kitchen to my cosy bed in the loft. This whole holiday had been action-packed and full of new places, faces and experiences, a mix upon which I continued to thrive. It was, at the same time, like all good breaks, a time of hiatus while everything stands still and body, mind and soul make ready for further adventures. South Bridge Primary School in Edinburgh awaited me.

My First Teaching Appointment

In the autumn of 1948 I began my work there. The establishment was in one of Edinburgh's poorest areas. The building had been condemned in 1913. Two wars later and three years more and it was still standing, full of great draughty classrooms with coal-fires and gloomy stairways and corridors tiled like a public lavatory! This was a difficult school and not, on the face of it, the best of places to start one's teaching career. Many years later, when eventually I went to university I read a paper about a 'black school', black because of its ethos. The 'inmates' were caught in a vicious circle. The children needed strong discipline which meant the liberal use of corporal punishment, and the more this was used the more discipline the children needed. No teacher dared break into this circle if he or she wanted to survive. South Bridge matched this pattern so well. It was a culture of deprivation, the school and the community which fed it. There was tremendous poverty and lack of amenities. Many fathers were in prison and women struggled to bring up large families against heavy odds. I had never experienced anything like this in all my practice teaching and it hit me with a tremendous sense of shock. The only teacher not to use a strap was a lady with a very caustic tongue, a weapon which seemed ten times worse. Each male teacher carried his strap all the time, fixed through his braces!

My first term was a nightmare, especially as my class of over forty ten-year-olds had just seen off their last teacher with a nervous breakdown! I looked with sympathy at the pile of comic papers in the cupboard, presumably used in an effort to keep the children quiet. Because this was what it was all about. If any real education went on it was a bonus! To add to my miseries there were the 'three musketeers' who ruled the ladies' staffroom with a rod of iron. Woe betide anyone who sat in the wrong chair or used the wrong mug! I was unfortunate enough to be in the classroom next to one of them, our rooms divided only by a movable partition. When the regimented silence in her place was disturbed by the active buzz in mine, she would think nothing of putting her disapproving face round the partition and asking petulantly for peace to work. I all but gave up the ghost until common sense asserted itself. My tutors at college had given me to understand that I would make a good teacher. I had very much enjoyed this part of my training and had good marks (perhaps why I had been appointed to this school!). I would learn to enjoy working in South Bridge and to my amazement I eventually did. Just when I began to win with that first class and how it was managed I cannot now recall. Perhaps it had something to do with the outings. I took groups of children to various places in the city. This was not then a common custom in Scotland. It had to be done on public holidays as any excursion out of the classroom was a waste of learning time!

On one occasion we went by tramcar, a new experience in itself to most of these children, to my beloved Braid Hills and had a campfire outside the cave which featured so much in my early life. I even had my first proposal of marriage sitting on a bench above it! Needless to say I did not share this memory with my class though perhaps if this had been today I would have done. How relationships have changed! Maybe in my own small way with this kind of event I was helping to change them. I was just saddened that day that half my class were unable to be with us as they were in the hands of the police for house-breaking. The headmaster had informed me the day before. He had also accepted the invitation sent by the children on my instigation, to join us at the picnic, and to the class's awed amazement, he came.

I began to meet the parents, visiting homes in dark, nauseous tenements. I listened to tales of the 'school-board', the colloquial name for the attendance officer, and co-operated to the best of my ability in affairs of truancy. There was one little fellow called Kelly with fair hair and brown eyes in an angelic face. He was constantly not with us and when he was he had to be carefully watched as he would nick the dinner

With children from South Bridge School,
Braid Hills, 1950

money when your back was turned, often at the same time quoting a
text from the Bible! I understand that his father had been converted in
prison by the Salvation Army. One day when Kelly was missing I
remember singing to the astonishment of my class, 'Has anybody here
seen Kelly?' in what I believed to be the manner of Florrie Ford, a well-
known Music Hall star, though her Kelly evoked a somewhat different
sentiment. It was a familiar song and the children obviously recognised
it. I think this was the first time that I was *quite* sure that the children
were laughing *with* me. It was a kind of breakthrough. I found my sense
of humour to be my greatest asset in this situation and we began to love
each other, the children and I.

Change of Schools

In my rebellion against the 'black school' regime, finding ways of
breaking into the vicious circle, I had incurred risk but it had paid off. I
was three years at South Bridge and my time there became gradually

more enjoyable. I learned such a lot. I only hope my pupils did too. There started for me a lifelong interest in the connection between social experience and school learning. In addition it was probably the start of my fascination with the place of language in learning, especially if the learning medium is foreign to the pupils. I was as Scottish as the South Bridge children but their 'language' was one I was not familiar with. For instance I could not understand why the children roared with laughter in a geography lesson when I told them that people in Ireland spoke Erse. I discovered that this was the South Bridge pronunciation of 'arse'! I shall always be grateful for my first job which dropped me in at the deep end so I quickly learned to 'swim'.

But I was soon to move on and it came about in an interesting way. On a Friday afternoon it was our onerous and tedious duty to work out the week's attendance percentage of our classes and to send our registers to the Deputy Head. He checked them and the class with the highest percentage was rewarded by being allowed to leave school early. If any teacher was late with this calculation the whole school might have to be 'kept in' and the offender was less than popular with both pupils and colleagues. Counting was never my best subject and I found this task a real headache. With a lively class in my care and all of us tired at the end of the week, it was even worse.

Then one Friday I was inspired. I told the children to fold a page in their jotter into a number of columns and to put, at the top of each, one of a group of letters e.g. 'ai', 'ee', 'ch', 'igh'. 'Take out of your desk any book you like including the Bible', I said, 'and find words with these patterns in them'. I said we would find out who had the most. It was a game that they seemed to enjoy and I had blessed silence for as long as I needed it. This became a regular Friday afternoon feature.

It was the pointer to the next step in my professional journey. I was to become what was known in Edinburgh at that time as an adjustment teacher. It was the day of the I.Q. (Intelligence Quotient') and the mental age of each child was worked out based on this. If tests in reading, spelling etc showed that a child was not 'working according to potential' then adjustment was needed. There was an adjustment teacher in each primary school who had no class of her own but who took groups from all the classes.

The South Bridge adjustment teacher had noticed a vast improvement in the test scores of the children from my class, in a short time. We eventually traced this to my Friday 'game'. Without my realising it this activity had given the children a new 'insight into pattern' as it came later to be called. With my colleague's encouragement my interest in special needs grew and eventually I became an adjustment teacher, helped by in-service training. I left South Bridge and went to Milton House, a little lower down the Royal Mile from Moray House. So I was once again in my old stamping-ground, the pupils very similar to those in South Bridge but the ethos of the school perhaps not quite so 'black'.

For two years I worked enjoyably as adjustment teacher in this school during which I was asked by the Authority to start adjustment work in St Ninian's, a Roman Catholic school. There were no Catholic adjustment teachers apparently. I would work three days in St Ninian's and the other two still in Milton House. It was a heavy assignment working in two schools mainly because of the added testing, reporting and general paper-work. But I welcomed the opportunity to work with Catholics. I discovered that they were 'normal' human beings like myself and all the fears and prejudices of my childhood disappeared. It was a further step towards my future career.

North Merchiston Club

During these early teaching years my concert work had continued, in both singing and drama. I even had private singing lessons for a time with Mona Benson, a fiery Russian lady who would have liked to make me into a 'dramatic singer' but I wanted only to sing for pleasure and I left her. In addition to my acting with Miss Allan's theatre group I belonged for a time to the Schools Theatre Company, a group of teachers who performed for school-children. And in 1951 I was approached, out of the blue, by the girls' leader at North Merchiston Club. Would I produce a play with the senior girls? The club was to take part in a drama festival. This I did and we won the cup much to my delight and amazement. I had become very attached to these girls and to the club in general. The whole notion of youth work was a new and exciting dimension for me. When the girls' leader left I took on her job which was paid. I worked three nights a week.

With girls' club members, 1951

It was a time of great expansion in this field and I was drawn into yet another world. I met and worked with some very dedicated people, including Stanley Nairne who was something of an institution. Like others of his generation he felt motivated to give his means and indeed his life to young people. He was a leading figure in the country where boys' clubs were concerned. He had started the North Merchiston Club before the war during which a girls' section was begun. By the 1950s this place was well known all over Scotland and I was proud to be a part of it.

Up-date of Current News and more 'Extra-curricular'

These events were happening between 1948 and 1953. Alex left school in 1951 as joint dux. Most Scottish schools used this word to mean the scholar with the highest marks. The dux of a secondary school was a prestigious position, normally meriting a medal and one's name on the Board of Honour. Alex had all this. He also gained fifth place in the University Bursary Competition. Joan moved into the Higher Grade at Gillespie's and Dorothy started school the year I began teaching. Family and church life went on and in the wider world the great powers divided up Berlin between them. We were still in the post-war period of 'a new beginning', still rationed for many commodities but revelling in the 'new look'! I was the proud possessor of a flared skirt - calf-length, which exemplified the notion. The austerity could be eased. Our life in Merchiston Park was enhanced by the comings and goings of more and more young friends as Alex and Joan brought their chums there and we were all roped in to help clear the leaves when our twenty two chestnut trees shed them in autumn, and chase the intruders looking for conkers and scrumping for fruit from our apple and pear trees. The large garden took some looking after.

My walking and cycling in the country continued with Alex and Mairi and others. Alex and I enjoyed one particular holiday in the Borders in spite of the rain, hiking for miles from hostel to hostel. I remember that one of these near Moffat later became a hotel where Alex and his new bride spent the first night of their honeymoon! In our hostelling days it had a horrible reekie stove, the scent of which lingered on our clothes for a long time.

In 1949 Mairi was spending a year in France as part of her university course in Modern Languages. I joined her for a while. This was my first excursion abroad and what a thrill it was! Mairi was so proud to introduce me to the sights in Paris and together, along with a friend Mairi had met there, we took a coach to the Riviera and enjoyed a short holiday in Cannes. I remember being somewhat ashamed of my grammar book French which did not take me very far amongst the French! The summer holiday of 1950 was one mad scamper. First I hitchhiked from Edinburgh to Land's End with May, a teacher friend met through the SCM Camp movement. That was quite an adventure. Travel costs for the whole journey were three shillings and eleven pence – in old money! After a short time in the Land's End area, May had to leave for the north again but I had more time and went over to the Isles of Scilly. I found a job on a bulb farm as my money was running out. From my vast experience of farming in Scotland, I managed to persuade this all-male establishment that I was well-qualified! I finally hitchhiked most of the way home from Cornwall and caught up with the family on their annual holiday at Belhaven. This was followed almost immediately by three weeks in the Netherlands with my musical friend Mary. We had only limited funds, and spent the last week sitting on the balcony watching the world go by on the canal and road below. We bought the most frugal of supplies and ate in our room much to the consternation of the hotel staff. Returning from Amsterdam I had another quick turn-around and flew (another first) to Northern Ireland where I had my initial experience of being an officer at an SCM camp. The place was Carnlough, north of Belfast and on the coast. It was cold and wet and fires had to be lit in the old house. This became one of my jobs! I remember the red mud of the Giant's Causeway, and the beauties of the Glens of Antrim even in the rain. That year it was a rest to get back to work!

And the holiday of 1951. I wrote a very full journal of this and wish there were time and space now to linger on it. I went on my own to Scandinavia. In Denmark I stayed with friends of Auntie Jean and Uncle Willie and in Sweden with friends of these friends. I learned how much better it is to live with people in their homes when you travel, if this is possible. I received such kindness and hospitality in all three countries. Again the Hostels Association came to my aid as I had no personal friends in the north of Sweden or Norway. Once more I was caught up in the camaraderie of the 'road', this time internationally, and in my growing interest in samenesses and differences the position of my own culture was seen in perspective. I was growing up.

Back to the Mainstream

The next two years were completely full of school and club. I loved it all and even found a boyfriend, also in the club movement. I also met Etta Hunter, a girls' club leader in another Edinburgh club. We became very good friends and used to talk late into the night. What with my onerous day-time work in two schools, my club work which in my enthusiasm took up almost every night, and the lack of sleep – my health began to suffer. I became very tired and had to go on a diet because of tummy trouble. Then I had a complete month off and took myself to Ostend for a holiday. This whole experience was a salutary lesson. I had learnt that even in my early twenties I was not indestructible and that I must attempt to pace myself better no matter how much I loved my work.

Perhaps I needed a complete change. It became clear that I could not continue to do both teaching and youth club work and I must choose. I very nearly went to Darroch Junior Secondary School where there was a post going for a teacher to 'adjust' those in the lower streams. Here, I thought, I would be able to combine my remedial teaching experience with that of my club-work. But it was not to be. Again, out of the blue or so it seemed to me, I was approached by St Katherine's Club and Community Centre in Aberdeen which required a Deputy Warden and Girls' Club Leader. There appeared to be a kind of inevitability about it, as though this challenging step had to be taken. I accepted the post and began work there in 1953 when I was twenty five. I had worked for five years in Edinburgh and was to stay for three in Aberdeen. To many and sometimes to myself, I seemed to be something of a rolling stone, but now, in hindsight, I realise that all these varied experiences were a kind of probation in so many ways for what was to follow.

Chapter 6

St. Katherine's Club and Community Centre

Lodgings

I enjoyed living in Aberdeen, the Granite City of the north-east. I found the Aberdonians very warm and welcoming and, once I got used to the dialect, I enjoyed their pawky humour. I lived in digs, the first of which I shared with a number of lodgers, including Archie Glen who played football for the Dons and was famous nationally. He eventually married the landlady's daughter in traditional manner! A particular memory of my stay in that house is my taking part in the Burns Supper organised by the Dons football fans. I gave the toast to Robert Burns, the Immortal Memory, and managed in my speech to have Burns playing football for the Dons. We had a lot of fun.

During the course of my time in the city I stayed in four different places, each etched in my memory for different reasons. There was my landlady in the Midstocket area who treated me like a daughter. I was her first and only lodger. I got to know her family too and often visited Crathes estate near Banchory where her son-in-law was factor. These good folks remained friends over the years. Sadly Mrs. Edwards died suddenly and I had to move on. I stayed temporarily in a hotel at the top of Union Street. The proprietor was a Polish gentleman who could speak many languages and was used as an interpreter in the courts when foreign trawler men were in trouble. He was a colourful character as indeed were several of his residents. I never did understand what went on in the attic rooms above me though I had my suspicions! My last 'home' was with an elderly single lady who took me in for company I suppose, though I was not at home very much. Miss Low was a great raconteur and would often regale me with her tales, especially of the royals and incumbents of the stately homes in the environs of Aberdeen.

Sunday lunch here was always steamed fish and mealy pudding, a very enjoyable combination.

The Club and Centre

The work I was called upon to do in St Katherine's was varied and certainly challenging. The warden, Mr Manson, had been recently appointed and he had a difficult job following a lady who was virtually a legend in the city. Like Stanley Nairne in Edinburgh, Bella Walker in Aberdeen gave everything she had, her education, her means, her health and above all her love and care to the establishment of a club. This was to serve the working girls of Aberdeen. She recruited a partner, Elsie Moffat, and together they built up a lively going concern which eventually, after several moves, gained purpose-built premises in West North Street. Changing times, and especially the Second World War, had their effect on this cosy girls' club. A boys' section was formed and then, as the youth grew into adults, various clubs for both men and women were established, one of them, the Eighteen Plus, being mixed. By the time I came on the scene the place had become a full-blown community centre with six hundred adult members and four hundred youth and apart from the fulltime warden and deputy, there were leaders of the various clubs, many of them voluntary and some from the membership itself. Add to this the classes which were run by the city council on weeknight evenings and the dances for all age-groups open to the public on Saturday evenings and you had a building humming with activity morning, noon and night seven days a week.

When I arrived in 1953 the organisation was already showing signs of strain. The change from an exclusive girls' club run by a benignly autocratic lady and her colleague, to a large general community centre with city involvement, was bound to cause a few hiccups, not the least on the financial side. There were various committees in which city dignitaries, staff and members met regularly to thrash out problems of policy and finance. I was quite bewildered at first by this maze of bureaucracy and I have to admit that I found it very tedious at times and the least enjoyable part of my new work. But, that being said, there began for me now a very full and stimulating programme which taxed all my energies and initiative, interestingly using and further developing many of the skills acquired in my Edinburgh work.

Deputy Warden and Girls' Club Leader

That was my official title. As Deputy Warden I was involved in the work of the whole centre, six women's clubs, two men's clubs and clubs for both boys and girls of all ages, including the mixed club for the eighteen plus. All this I shared with the warden but his role tended to be more administrative while mine took me into the club-work itself. Also I had much more contact with the women's clubs in particular. As a girls' club leader I was a kind of supervisor of a number of very competent young women who led the various clubs direct. There was a male part-time supervisor who did the same on the boys' side. This constituted the core of my work, not forgetting the night classes and the Saturday dances, each with their own organisers but still part of our community. The clubs met every week. Each adult club had its own committee, in theory at least, and ran its own programme but very often if a speaker did not come or the member running a games session didn't turn up, I found myself being prevailed upon to fill in. The cupboard in my office became a repository of ideas and equipment for ready-made programmes. The work I had done at North Merchiston was useful, especially the Scottish country dancing, singing and drama and the recitations of my concert work served to entertain. I soon learned how to organise beetle drives and other games.

There were also the special events for the whole centre such as a St. Andrew's Night or a Burns Supper when it was a matter of all hands on deck. A huge annual fair known as the Members' Effort helped to keep the whole ship afloat financially. In a sense each Saturday was a special event too because it was an open night. Many non-club members simply paid to come in. There was modern dancing in the big hall to a local band, sequence dancing in a smaller hall for the older folks and dancing of a kind! for the young teens in the recreation room or 'wreck' as it was affectionately known. There would be several hundred people in the building at that time with one of the front offices used as a ticket cloakroom.

The canteen was a problem for me. Somehow it had fallen to me to make sure that it was adequately staffed on Saturdays by club members. I recruited in the regular clubs during the week and the volunteers were mostly women. Sometimes the warden or myself had to help here if we were short but it was better that we should be free to roam the premises. We worked alternate Saturdays. On the whole we had few problems other than a certain boisterousness, which occasionally became rowdyism if people came in after visiting the pub opposite, an establishment referred to by locals as the 'hairy bar'.

Memorable Times

But I do remember two incidents in particular, which raised my blood pressure slightly. The first took place in the large dance hall. I had noticed certain lads in each corner of the room, nonchalantly leaning against the wall and not taking part in the dancing. Jimmy, one of the club members, warned me that there might be trouble, as he knew this 'gang' were out to 'get him' for some reason. I asked the bandleader to announce a lady's choice and I danced Jimmy as far as the hall door where I was forced to leave him as the gang had gathered and a fracas began. Adults from the sequence dancing opposite had also spilled out into the crush-hall and joined the melee. I ran through the crowd to the phone in my office. The police were in Lodge Walk at that time, very near. They came at once knowing that I would not call them unless it was really necessary, by which time the gang had fled, guessing my intention. But I was able to point the police in their direction and gave silent thanks that no arrests would now be made on our premises.

The second dicey moment I remember vividly involved trawler-men. Aberdeen's fishing industry was at its height in those days and St. Katherine's was not far from the docks. One Saturday night when I was in the canteen I noticed a young fisherman weaving somewhat uncertainly across the room with a tray of soft drink bottles in his hands. He joined his party of lads and girls leaving a trail of liquid on the floor. I brought a bucket and mop and asked the fellow politely to clean up. He rose to his full six foot something with the mop in his hand whilst his party backed away and made a circle round us. My heartbeat had quickened and I visualised myself at any moment on the end of that mop!

'I work so many hours a day etc.', my bold opponent began and I interrupted to inform him that the workers in the canteen were voluntary and not there to clean up after him. He then demanded to see the manager and when I said he was speaking to her he asked to see me 'private like'. So I led him along to my office, which was near the front door. The gentleman who was the boxing trainer was the 'bouncer' that night and offered help but I declined it and prayed I would be able to cope. As soon as my trawler-man was away from his mates he 'collapsed' and apologised. It was his birthday and they were celebrating, first in the pub and then at the dancing. He offered to clean up but when we returned to the canteen his friends had done it for him. I wasn't going to let him off the hook entirely however, and had him collecting empty bottles which he did quite meekly. On looking back, these incidents plus times when our centre was mistaken for the working-man's club in the next block and we had the occasional unwelcome visitor, were very innocuous compared with the drug-related and other misdemeanours that police and social workers have to deal with today. Even on New Year's Eve, the traditional party time of the Scots when we might have six hundred people on the premises, the mood of the crowd was good humoured as they lined up at the 'bottle cloakroom' to collect their seasonal 'bit of warmth' at midnight, prior to first-footing, the traditional visiting to wish good luck in the New Year.

Speaking of this brings another memory vividly to mind. The weeks around Christmas were my most hectic time. I might have to attend at least fourteen Christmas parties. By the New Year I felt I never wanted to see jelly and mince pies ever again! Then I had my holiday. I caught an early train to Edinburgh on New Year's morning. I slept the night at St. Katherine's, curled up on a sofa in the lounge used as the accountant's office, one of the few rooms not strewn with the debris of the night and the only one furnished with a couch. The caretaker, whose flat was on the top floor, would see me into my 'bedroom' and then lock up. It was weird lying in the silent darkness when so recently all had been noisy merriment and light. I had a warm sleeping bag against the intense cold of the Aberdeen winter's night. I remember the caretaker saying, 'If you hear any strange noises, Miss Garvie, just give a shout and I'll lock my door'! Somehow I slept and somehow I got up in time for my train, washed in cold water, ate something and got myself to the station. I was healthy and still in my twenties. I was tired but happy. Life was full of purpose.

Warden

Things were never quite the same after I was persuaded, against my will, to become Warden. Mr. Manson left for personal reasons. A new deputy was appointed, Ron Giles, and a new post created, that of Assistant Warden. This was filled by Mary Pickstone. They were lovely people and we were a grand team, I the youngest and the other two both highly qualified and experienced in club-work. I learned much from them. But the move to administration was not for me. I much preferred the practical person-to-person work of the club leader in the front line as it were. However I continued for some time though I gradually became very tired as I tried to do both the office work and the club work, which I so much enjoyed, no doubt poaching on the ground of my assistants.

But there *are* some good memories of this time. For instance I was able to develop my involvement in the spiritual side of the centre. At the heart of the building was a small and very attractive chapel. Bella Walker had linked her work to the Young Women's Christian Association and every club meeting still had its time of worship though the actual YWCA membership was now restricted to a small group. The chapel was a very special place, simply but beautifully furnished. I remember in particular the lovely panelling and the little harmonium which I enjoyed trying to play though I was an indifferent performer. From the start of my time in St. Katherine's I had led worship for the various clubs, but now, released a little from the busyness of the club programmes, I developed these chapel sessions. I found myself giving more and more time to the preparation. The prayers reflected our community and its needs as the club members shared their lives with me. Of course I respected privacy but I learned in a very real way that where two or three are gathered together God is in the midst and that group prayer can sustain the individual. There was something important and right I felt when for example a group of teenagers which a moment before had been making itself felt in no uncertain manner, calmly sat in the quiet of this lovely oasis and considered their Maker for a brief span. I enjoyed finding the relevant thing to say. I cannot now remember the detail of my homilies but I suppose, for the young ones at least, they would have had something of the Head's talks at school assembly mixed with those of the Sunday-school teacher. My previous experience had a bearing just as this was to influence my later life. I did worry sometimes that the club chapel for many members was taking the place of church. I was very humbled and somewhat troubled when a mother asked me to baptise her baby. Perhaps I could and should have done it but I referred her to the church next door whose minister was our official chaplain and where I myself was a member though I hardly ever got there because of my Sunday work. I don't think the lady ever went to the church. At that time I was not deeply concerned about the matter but perhaps this was the start of my questioning in later life. What *is* the church and how important are professional clergy? Was this a precursor of my Quaker future?

Club Holidays

Another aspect of the work, which I was able to indulge more when I became Warden was the club holiday and time out. I organised a number of these and went on some myself. There were the holidays at Kilmory Castle, at that time one of a number of holiday centres for young people in Britain. It lies in one of the loveliest parts of Argyllshire. I had taken a party from North Merchiston Club and now I took the St. Katherine's members. The two met up on more than one occasion. There was a resident warden but most groups had their own leaders and, rain or shine, we always found interesting things to do.

The holidays in the centre's house in Persley Den were an on-going part of the summer programme, each club booking its time. I visited frequently and occasionally stayed for a while. Then there were the one-off camps, picnics, days away. A memorable week in Glass on the borders of Banffshire, for junior children comes vividly back. I remember being saddened when I found that some of these city children didn't know what to do with the glorious freedom of the wide-open spaces. Then I remembered my South Bridge pupils and our day out on the hills. It was my privilege to introduce them to a new richness. Although for me this was officially part of my job, it was such a wonderful part. To share time out and to use that time not only for exploring new places and enjoying leisure activities but for close companionship of a very special kind was to bring great joy. I also experienced a particular learning event for myself. I was able to attend a Scottish/Danish summer-school in Denmark, sponsored by social services. For me it was a return visit to this attractive country and on this occasion I found out more about its history and culture along with those of Scotland! I found myself teaching Scottish dancing. It was interesting too to see something of the work being done in community centres there and to learn of their truly advanced projects.

End of Another Experience

By 1956 I felt that my time at St. Katherine's was running out. I was missing teaching, the thing I had been trained for, much as I loved club work. Also I had had more than enough of administration. Wrestling with policy and financial problems was not my field. I felt instinctively that the place was in the early stages of anachronism. Times were changing a decade after the war and all the hectic efforts to keep up the membership and to raise funds seemed to me, exhausted by them, to be rather like flogging a dead horse. The place needed a new purpose and regime. But I resigned with very mixed feelings – tiredness – sadness – relief – but above all perhaps a sense of gratitude for the opportunity to be part of what had been a great institution.

Chapter 7

St. Denis School

Breathing Space

I returned to Edinburgh. The family still lived at Merchiston Park. Alex had gone to University in Edinburgh and had left with a first in Classics. He was to go to Cambridge to do the Tripos but first served in the army for the statutory two years, including a spell in trouble-torn Cyprus interpreting for the British army. This was an anxious time for us as many British personnel were losing their lives in the Cyprus conflict but, thank God, Alex survived to go to Cambridge. Joan had qualified in business studies and was now in office work. She was an enthusiastic Tawny Owl in her Brownie pack. Dorothy was still at Gillespie's, doing well and aspiring to nursing. As for me, my mother had spotted an advertisement for a primary teacher wanted in St. Denis School for girls, an independent day and boarding school very near Merchiston Park. The teacher would be required to cover for a member of staff who had leave of absence for one term. It seemed just right. A term would give me breathing space. I applied and was successful. It was during the 1950s that both Gran and Grandma died (we had lost our grandfathers in 1938 and 1942 respectively). This was a very special kind of ending for our family. It was also so in a wider sense or perhaps it was just that I became aware of it then. I read Nevil Shute's book, 'On the Beach'. I had read most of his books and saw him as something of a prophet. This book therefore dismayed me greatly as it told of nuclear war. It was the first time I had really thought much about this horror. I always recall the period as the end of the post-war euphoria and the start of the nuclear nightmare. I became conscious of the numerous 'Ban-the-Bomb' campaigns and I joined something called 'One-in-Five', a group of women who pledged themselves to learn all about the possible survival techniques. From then on every conflict in the world was looked at with trepidation lest it escalate into nuclear war. The Suez crisis was one of these when

Prime Minister Anthony Eden somewhat disgraced himself. Russia and the United States were in constant confrontation and the Cold War had begun.

Day Teacher

As things turned out I was to be at St. Denis for four years. A permanent junior school post had become vacant and I was offered it. I accepted and for two years was a day teacher. Then the post of housemistress of the middle school boarding-house became vacant and the headmistress asked if I was interested. Sensing yet another exciting challenge I applied for this and again was successful. But I jump ahead.

Being in Edinburgh again allowed me to link up with Mairi once more and Alex when he was at home. I renewed acquaintance with the Braid and Pentland Hills and Mairi and I had a glorious holiday in the Rhineland in 1957. That year also I became a godmother for the first time, to my cousin Doris' son, Michael. In 1958 I enjoyed a lovely holiday in Switzerland with a fellow teacher.

I was again immersed in church affairs attending College Church with the family. I sang in the choir, attended social events and took a place again on the congregational board. I also became an adherent of the West End churches which at that time had as their incumbents some of the finest preachers in Scotland. I went on Sunday evening and occasionally found myself queuing to get in! Ministers like William Barclay were a lasting inspiration. During the first two years at St. Denis, at least there was time again for musical evenings at home. With Mary at the piano, Alex playing his violin, Dad and I singing and sometimes uncles and other family members taking their parts, we whiled away many a happy evening. I did more concert work particularly in the Portobello area where Uncle Willie was still running entertainment for his old people. The Burns Supper continued to be an important event. My interest in the bard even got me into adjudicating a festival on the outskirts of Edinburgh, a traumatic experience for me if not for the participants!

The School Community

St. Denis School was a happy community and I made many friends amongst staff, pupils and parents. The school at that time had about four hundred and fifty girls from five to eighteen years, of whom one third were boarders.It was accommodated in four large houses linked by their gardens which were beautifully kept by Docherty, the caretaker-cum-handyman. His wife was in charge of the indoor domestic staff, most of the maids being girls from the western isles. They used their Gaelic to great advantage! The Dochertys lived above the old coach house and were quite an institution, a kind of stabilising force as other staff came and went. The headmistress was Jessie Ramsay who had been a tutor at Moray House College when I was a student. She was a down-to-earth Scottish teacher, full of common sense, popular with pupils and parents and very supportive of staff. She was a lover of all things Scottish so we had Burns Suppers and concerts and dances with a Scottish flavour. There was the senior school dance when the girls brought male escorts, many of the boys wearing the kilt. The lads from Merchiston Castle School where our girls had brothers, wore the kilt as part of their uniform and the St. Denis girls wore tartan skirts as part of theirs. But the dance occasion saw the girls in long dresses. The evening was conducted with old-fashioned courtesy and decorum and gave a taste of gracious living. Indeed all the school events including sports, concerts and speech days seem to me in retrospect to have exuded a sense of happy social occasion.

It was towards the end of my second year as a day teacher in the junior school that the head dropped her bombshell. Would I be interested in becoming housemistress of the middle house (girls aged 12-16)? The present matron was retiring. I was highly flattered to be asked but somewhat dismayed when I considered all the implications. It would mean living in. There would be a fair amount of administration, not my favourite thing. I should also be required to know something about nursing and the treatment of minor ailments. I did have a Junior Red Cross certificate! But I was given to understand that the main requirement was the ability to get along with young people and to help to provide a home from home. This was less daunting in the light of my club experience.

Housemistress

So I became housemistress or matron of Ettrick, the middle house. I had thirty two girls in my care. My assistant, was Miss Young. We were very formal in Scotland in those days and it was a long time before I knew her first name. She had been there for some time and was able to show me the ropes. She had a lot of nursing experience. Also there was a fully qualified nurse in the junior house and the school doctor was extremely helpful and understanding. Unlike my predecessor and the matrons of the junior and senior houses, I was a *teaching* housemistress, keeping my work in the junior school part-time. I also taught religious education in the senior school. The rest of my time was devoted to the house. Gone was that breathing space of the past two years. I was once again fully immersed with very little time to call my own. Any changes I would wish to make in the regime of the house must be introduced gradually. For instance I began to visit the dormitories after the girls were in bed, spending a little time in each and sharing thoughts and prayer. These became precious moments of contact. It was particularly useful to do this near holiday-time. I would take round a large sheet of paper with headings like 'train', 'sandwiches', 'taxi' etc. I reckoned I might soon be qualified to apply for a job as a travel agent! When end of term came there was a tremendous flurry of activity with several taxis going off to train or bus station or airport, besides family cars. The three boarding-houses combined plans. On one famous occasion the taxis did not turn up but somehow, using cars of members of staff, we got all our charges away. The last girl to go from my house was a real 'St. Trinian's' lass. Miss Young took her to the station in a mad scramble to catch the train. She had me laughing helplessly on her return at the picture of the child being thrust aboard, clutching hockey stick and numerous bits and pieces as the train moved out. An astonished railway official was left staring at the contents of a tin which had been dropped. They were rather like those of a small boy's pocket. The girl at that time was twelve, very arty, completely feckless but very lovable.

Play and Work

We had fun at St. Denis, especially if the 1st of April fell in term time. For many years I kept a set of drawings done by a wag who was a talented cartoonist. She mounted her pictures on the wall which marked my route to the bathroom when I got up. She had me in various stages of 'coming to' with suitable captions. This was the one day of the year when everyone was up early. At least I never had to deal with staff being kidnapped and released only when demands were met, as I understand happened in Merchiston Castle School. Another fun time was Guy Fawkes night. Docherty always made a life-size guy. Normally the fellow met his end (the guy, not Docherty) on the bonfire but one year a serious drought meant that fires were prohibited. My imaginative pupils found another place for him. I came back after my evening off to find boots sticking out of my bed. Guy Fawkes was reclining there. Then I saw the squib pushed through the hook of the mirror above the fireplace. I never locked my door and I cannot remember any other occasion when the girls went in. My sense of humour took over and I roused Miss Young to come and enjoy the joke. Sadly the girls had been unable to keep awake. There was no way that I could go to sleep with that man in my room so between us Miss Young and I got him downstairs. We propped him up on the pantry side of the kitchen hatch and made sure we were on hand to enjoy the cook's shout of astonishment when she raised the hatch in the morning. She in turn put him on the toilet seat in the maids' lavatory! A few Gaelic shrieks announced *their* discovery. I have no recollection of the guy's final destination but I expect Docherty found some legitimate way of disposing of him.

But, lest the reader thinks that life at St. Denis was all fun and games, let me focus now on one or two more serious memories. There was an excellent teaching staff and the academic level was high. Many of the girls went on to do important things in life. It was good for me to be back in teaching and in such a congenial environment. The mostly very supportive parents meant that the children were highly motivated and the small classes allowed for almost individual tuition. It was all very rewarding. The work in my religious education classes gave rise to some interesting experiences. I recall one or two lively discussions with the sixth form particularly, concerning Paul's ideas about women. The discussion even spilled over into a weekend away. I took the girls to a youth hostel in the Borders. This was a very new thing for these young women, meeting and sharing living with those from a totally different background. One of my group was Hannah Gordon who later became a well-known actress and television personality. I recall with some

Hostelling, St Denis 6th Form, 1958.
Hannah Gordon is on extreme left, front row.

amusement the faces of the hostel warden and his wife when they found the entire community of the hostel having a short epilogue in the common room before bed. A St. Denis girl had played the piano and we had danced and sung, joined by the other hostellers. The time of prayer seemed a fitting end to the fun and the roughest of lads went off quietly to bed. I shared a dormitory with my pupils and there was a wonderful sense of fellowship. With a younger class I attempted to put something of my religious lessons into practice and had them making up Christmas parcels and taking them to needy old people whose names I got from Social Services. Again this took us into a different social scene. Dark stairs in seedy streets, small cluttered rooms none too clean, were foreign to my well-heeled pupils. Needless to say I wrote to the parents explaining the project and I had wholesale support. I was happy to learn that one or two of the girls kept up with their old people after this particular venture ended.

'St. Denis' attended St. Cuthbert's Church in the West End. The minister was our school padre. We went to both the morning and evening services and had our special pews in the gallery. Bed-time on Sunday was later after hot cocoa in winter and a cold drink in summer. My Sunday on duty was one night when I had to organise the drinks and, in winter, fill innumerable hot water bottles from a large urn in the kitchen. It was quite an exhausting hour.

Another 'pressure' point was the treatment session. At a certain time each day, both morning and evening, a hand bell was rung and either Miss Young or myself would be stationed in the bathroom where the first aid equipment was kept. Girls who needed attention were either treated there and then or referred to higher beings. The decision was often difficult but I always erred on the safety side, being very conscious that these were other people's children and that I was responsible for their well-being. I did, however, become fairly adept at sussing out reluctant school attenders. It was surprising how many sore tummies or headaches appeared at the time of a French test for instance!

Nursing Duty

In the second term of my first year as matron I was plunged into the 'deep end' when a bad strain of influenza hit the community at large and St. Denis in particular. The sick room was in the junior house and it was full to overflowing. So we had to manage somehow in the ordinary dormitories. For a time I had to give up teaching and concentrate on nursing. I wore a white coat with my thermometer in the top pocket. Temperatures had to be taken night and morning and my charts shown to the doctor who visited daily. I set up a nursing table in the middle of the landing where bottles of 'the mixture' and other things needed were placed in readiness, including at one stage a record player for entertaining those recuperating. Some of the girls were really very ill. With a few the illness became gastric and one suffered with severe earache. Several were ill more than once. The doctor prescribed the necessary drugs and explained everything very carefully to me. I had to watch the age of my patient, one dosage for older and another for younger, and keep very meticulous records. Miss Young and I consulted frequently.

For some reason, probably the same as affected the doctor, neither Miss Young nor myself caught the virus. It seemed that we were so exposed to it that we had built up an immunity. I did however suffer from a nasty eye infection as soon as term ended. I was just so tired. For, not only did the flu go on all term but there was also an appendix case and a tonsillectomy. Another little job was organising the hospital-visiting roster. This was of course after all the negotiating with parents/guardians in the first place. Did they want a private nursing home etc.? There seemed no end to the whirlwind of activity.

Trip to Paris

In the spring of 1960 we took a party of older girls to Paris, both day girls and boarders. I was one of five members of staff and the one responsible for the health of the party. The youngest of our group was asthmatic and had to be carefully watched. Fortunately, apart from a minor scare at the end of the holiday when this girl's temperature rose slightly, we were blissfully free of troubles. The main problem was a boys' school from Portsmouth with which we shared a hotel. The communicating doors in the corridors seemed to become mysteriously unlocked and it was necessary for me and my colleagues to patrol in the night watches.

A very poignant memory of this full and exciting week was our visit to the flat of Donald Caskie, a Scottish clergyman who had helped many during the Second World War to escape from the Nazis. He was known as the Tartan Pimpernel. Our headmistress knew him personally and he had invited us to meet him. The apartment was full of flowers, with plants trailing over the balcony railings, and the strong scent of lilac pervades my memory of our time with this quiet-spoken, humble man who was such a war hero. None of us would ever forget him.

We visited most of the main Paris sights. We teachers kept eagle eyes on our charges as we walked the boulevards and travelled by metro. How thankful we were that we had insisted on uniform. The girls were all in their familiar green with the tartan Sunday-wear skirt. So they were distinctive. There was one location which is probably not a usual tourist attraction and that is the school set up by Napoleon for the daughters of his officers and appropriately called St. Denis. We *had* to go there. It was still functioning then as a boarding school. Our girls decided that St. Denis, Edinburgh was not so bad after all! We were all appalled at some of the conditions, the long dormitories sleeping about fifty girls each with a 'cabinet' for the teacher in the centre. I very nearly

Paris, 1960. St. Denis party outside City Hall.
Donald Caskie, in front row, third from right,
and Headmistress, Jessie Ramsay fourth from right.

had to stay behind with the asthmatic pupil whose temperature had gone up suddenly on the eve of departure but she recovered sufficiently to travel and we all made our way to the boat together. There were about seven hundred children and their teachers on the ship and they were nearly all sick as it was an extremely choppy crossing. I ended up organising a singsong on one deck to keep heads up. I was rather glad to see the white cliffs of Dover.

More Memories

But I had little time to recover. The new term was upon us and as always house staff had to go in ahead of the others, mainly to arrange any changes in the dormitory places and bathroom rosters. Even the staff had to learn to stick to their times for baths etc. A fifteen minute allotment can be real discipline. What a lot of lessons my St. Denis experience had given me and in such variety! Something else I began to understand is that social problems are not restricted to the 'have-nots'. I well remember the sense of shock when I overheard a girl in my house saying to her father on the phone, 'Oh by the way Daddy, did you know that Mummy is in hospital?' The parents were divorced as so many were. Because there was money the children could be looked after at boarding-school. But I came to recognise the same traumas I had met in my early teaching, the effects of instability in the home and a sense of rootlessness. These are the same whether father is on the dole or a millionaire.

But, to finish on a lighter note, our Gaelic-speaking maids were allowed occasionally to use the telephone in my sitting room. I did try to keep out when they were phoning but sometimes it was necessary to go to my desk urgently. The maids used Gaelic so they felt 'safe'. One evening I had left the radio on after listening to the news. I had forgotten to turn it off. The English version had given way to that in Gaelic. A maid went in to phone and I heard later that they were all very troubled. Did Miss Garvie understand Gaelic and what had they been saying? I never did enlighten them.

The Next Step

I had been at St. Denis four years when the head surprised me again by asking if I had ever thought of teacher training as a job. I hadn't, but did now, coupled with a notion I had had since my time in the Girls' Association, that of working overseas. This idea had never gone away. In discussion with my G.A. friend, Irene, I had seen myself as a possible church missionary, so long as I could also carry on with my acting! My parents were not so sure and I had put the notion on the back burner, as it were. My parents were still doubtful. If I must go overseas there were other lines I could take. I am sure that their doubts were not because of the missionary work itself. As church people they had a great respect for missionaries. It was probably more to do with their understanding of me as a person. They could not see me in the role, just as when I was leaving school and had indicated my interest in going on the stage professionally, they had not felt this was right. Much as they were convinced by my enthusiasm and recognised some talent they did not see me as a full-time thespian. Perhaps my father's recollection of actor lodgers in his early home had something to do with this. Be that as it may, they made enquiries on my behalf at the Royal Academy of Dramatic art in London. I am not sure what this revealed but whatever it was they were strongly influenced by my headmistress who persuaded them that teaching would be the right way forward and so it was.

Missionary – actress – teacher – all possible and tempting and of course not mutually exclusive. For example, one could be a missionary teacher and one could teach drama and of course use it as a teaching technique. For me, the *main* road was to be teaching, the others important parallel tracks. I shall always be grateful that through the people who knew and loved me God was guiding. It was my mother, once again, who found the advert. An Education Officer was required in Uganda which at that time was still a British protectorate. Applications should be made to the Colonial Office. I can almost hear Mum's resigned sigh as she pointed it out. The adrenalin began to pump once more. Encouraged by both parents and colleagues I applied and was successful. My 'apprenticeship' in Scotland was over and life in the big wide world about to begin.

Chapter 8

Run-up to 'Uganda'

Family Holiday

I left St. Denis at the end of the summer term, 1960. I was due to sail on the S.S. Uganda in September so I had just under two months to prepare mind and soul and material luggage. It was all very exciting. I did manage to join the family on holiday in Grantown-on-Spey, a new place for us all and very lovely. But it rained heavily for almost the whole of the two weeks. The fishers of the Spey had the best time of all. When not trudging in the rain or going to the cinema which changed its programme three times a week, I made use of enforced captivity in the hotel to learn Swahili which was the lingua franca of East Africa and would be useful. So I curled up with 'Teach Yourself Swahili' and let the world go by.

Another powerful memory of that holiday was my mother's bitter disappointment when a letter came telling us that the house (another in Braid Road) which we had 'put in for', had slipped from us, no doubt for a better offer. Mother was devastated. She had gone to the length of planning the curtains! Father was soon to retire and we would have to leave Merchiston Park. In the event he was allowed to keep the house for a while and it was 1964 before the family finally moved. It was a good holiday for Alex and me. He had completed his tripos in Cambridge, repeating his Edinburgh success with a 'first' and was to start as a lecturer in Greek at Glasgow University in the autumn. The girls were on other ploys though they joined us for part of the time.

Austrian memories and Malvern Camp Alex and I enjoyed our time together as always, going for walks in spite of the rain. We recalled the brief fun-time we had had the summer before when we met and had one night together in Innsbruck. It was the start of an Austrian holiday for me and a transit trip for Alex from Germany to Greece. Alex needed German and other languages for his Greek research and he went on courses and travelled a fair bit. We had much in common although along different lines, and an empathy which had never waned. I cannot resist recording both a laugh and a tear from the Innsbruck experience.

After a happy night of walking and singing in the hills above the town the morning came all too soon. I went to the station to see Alex off to Greece.

We had packed him a picnic and as he climbed aboard the night express, the badly packed parcel came apart and rolls bounced along the platform. How we laughed at our typical practical ineptness! This we certainly shared! We also shared a few tears, Alex as he plunged into the tunnel towards Yugoslavia and I as I made my lonely way back to my hotel. In a sense it was practice for the bigger farewell to come. In retrospect it seems to me that several happenings in the period prior to my departure for Uganda were pointers and preparatory experiences. Another was my last SCM 'camp' for schoolgirls at The Wells School in Malvern where I was Chaplain or Camp Leader. It had a very special ethos which is difficult to describe. The team of officers of several different Christian denominations welded so well together, quicker than I had ever known it happen. In the joy and peace of this situation I remember standing one evening at the window of my room and looking across the wide valley. I had a kind of vision of another place and a similar sensation of rightness. This was before I knew that I was going to Uganda. The vision was to be made real.

Change of Travel Plan

I am not sure when exactly the letter came form the Uganda administration but I was faced quite suddenly with a change of plan. Someone in Uganda had decided that it might be a good idea if I did some study on Teaching English as a Foreign Language. Would I please register with the course at the London Institute of Education and cancel my passage on the ship in September. I was to go to London for one term only and sail in December on the Kenya Castle of the Union Castle line. It seemed that I had no choice in the matter. I did what I was told and so found myself with an extra month in Edinburgh as the university term did not begin until October. It was useful time as it allowed me to do a short refresher course in infant methods at Moray House and to prepare my packing in a more leisurely way. A great deal of thought and planning had to go into this and I had much support from family and friends. The dining room table at Merchiston Park became the repository for the household items. I began to feel like a bride-to-be with her show of presents, a bride without a bridegroom! I wonder now, looking back, if I thought seriously about this. Here was I at 32 setting out for yet another very full-time life. Had I consciously or unconsciously decided that marriage and children were not for me? I think the truth is that I never really thought about it at all. I had had a number of boyfriends even during my school days and three proposals of marriage that I can remember. I enjoyed the company of men but for some reason my work and my career had always come first. When I was in Aberdeen I was being pursued by a young minister of the kirk. Several friends had seen me as a minister's wife and I really did think this might be 'it'. My beau had come to St. Katherine's and observed me at work. He was going to another church elsewhere and had envisaged me in his manse! Like my mother at Grantown-on-Spey I had got to the stage of planning the curtains. To my amazement rather than consternation, I have to confess, my pursuant eventually informed me that I would make 'a rotten minister's wife'. I would run both the kirk and the minister! So that was that. Perhaps God was trying to tell me something.

One of the people who helped me a great deal during this time of preparation was Jean Gray who had been a club member and youth club leader at St. Katherine's. She had kept in touch with me throughout my St. Denis days and often visited me in Edinburgh. Jean was a professional tailoress, later to become head of tailoring in one of Aberdeen's most prestigious shops. She gave me good advice on my wardrobe and we enjoyed shopping together for clothes we considered suitable for the tropics and for all occasions.

The London Course and a Taste of Russia and Wales

At last it was time to go to London, with a new date for my sailing. I was now booked on the S.S. Kenya Castle for the 23rd of December with the prospect of having both Christmas and New Year at sea. Unknown to me the powers that be in Uganda had acted unilaterally in this matter of the English course and my employer, the Colonial Office, was very put out it seemed. My first weeks in London were spent in having to explain why I had altered my travel plans and that I needed some money to cover my London expenses. This was normally allowed for overseas staff doing recommended courses but the suddenness of the change of plan had taken everyone by surprise. The left hand did not know what the right hand did. It was eventually sorted out and I settled to my three months of study and my taste of university life. I acquired digs with a Miss Brander at Parliament Hill Fields near Highgate and learned to commute on the Northern Line of the underground like a true Londoner. At that time in my life I found all this very exciting. Just to be in London and enjoy its amenities was a special thing in itself. Apart from one other, the people in my class were all from overseas. I became very friendly with a Russian lady who taught English in Moscow. She also was on the course for only one term. When we parted she thrust presents on me and embraced me in warm Russian style. I have often wondered how far our friendship could have gone if circumstances had been different. This was the height of the Cold War.

I enjoyed my studies. To look at one's language with the eyes of a foreigner is enormously enlightening. So many windows are opened. Not only was I acquiring the techniques of teaching English as a foreign language but I was also learning about language per se. It was part of my lasting interest in means of communication linked to the cultures in which language operates. For a short period we were sent to North Wales to practise teaching in a non-English-speaking area. I stayed with the Thomases at the end of the windy causeway in Pwhelli, battling my way in the November gales as I returned each day from my little country school in the village of Edern. Ina, my Russian friend, lived nearby as did a few of the African students, each of us assigned to a different school in the vicinity. The rest of the class were all stationed somewhere along the rail route from England. Apparently this was an annual invasion which the local people enjoyed very much.

My school was the village primary. In theory the education offered was bilingual – Welsh/English – but in effect it seemed to me that it was very Welsh. I loved this and endeavoured to learn a few words of Welsh. At the same time I enjoyed putting my new-found skills into practice. I discovered how much language can be acquired through games – singing – story and so many of the activities appropriate for young children. I began to see something of the richness of culture and its linguistic expression. I became interested in comparing Welsh and English and noting samenesses and differences, an exercise which was to stand me in good stead in years to come as I worked with people of many cultures.

I tried to make the most of this short Welsh experience and I look now at the photograph of me wearing a high Welsh hat, a child on each

A Welsh experience

hand, and a hundred memories come flooding back. I even learned something of Communist Russia as I 'vetted' Ina's excellent English. She was in a secondary school and had been asked to read a paper on the then five year plan for her country. In spite of telling myself firmly that Ina had asked me to vet her English and not her politics, I found myself arguing until 2.00 a.m. Her grandmother had been a Christian but what had God done for Russia?! Ina was an ardent communist. If she had not been she would never have been allowed to come to Britain.

Leaving Home

We returned to London and the end of term saw me back in Edinburgh and busy with last-minute packing. There were three categories of luggage, things to go in the hold not wanted on voyage, others in a more accessible place which might be wanted from time to time, and the things to go in the cabin for immediate and continual use. It all required careful planning. So busy and happy was I that I never gave much thought to what my family and friends must have been feeling. I was going away and my contract was initially for three years. It was only in the actual parting that this came home to me. I was to go to London by night-train. The ship left from Tilbury and Alex was to come all the way to the dock with me. His sleeping compartment was on the same corridor in the train. My parents, sisters and other relatives came to the station at Edinburgh to see me off as did my good friend, Mairi. The one most upset, it seemed to me, was Dad. The tears were flowing. I was strangely calm but relieved when the whistle finally blew and we were away. But my fitful sleep was disturbed just after the train left Berwick-upon-Tweed. The steward apologised for troubling me but had seen my light still on and felt that he should convey the message he had just received. I had left my tickets and passport in Edinburgh! How could this possibly be? All my important documents were in my briefcase, a posh leaving present from St. Denis with my initials on the front. But where was the briefcase? It was nowhere to be seen. I began to panic but was assured by the kindly steward that arrangements had been made for the case to be brought to London on a later train and I would be able to pick it up there. It would be in the care of the guard.

How on earth had this happened? Then I remembered. Dad had taken the briefcase to hold while I got myself settled in the compartment with the rest of my luggage. In his distress he had gone on holding it and none of us noticed! I dared not think of what happened next. I learned later that Mairi had taken charge. The family were too upset to think straight. She had gone to the station-master and made all the arrangements. I shall never know the details but will remain eternally grateful for the help I received. The case duly turned up in London and we all got on with our lives! It had been a very troubled night for everyone except Alex who knew nothing about it till morning. For me it was a lesson in carefulness. I learned to check the number of pieces in my hand luggage a lot more scrupulously. Poor Dad had to say goodbye yet again when I phoned to re-assure him that all was well and that the fault was mine.

One of the perks of this Colonial Office job was a year's membership of the Royal Overseas League. The London club-house is in Park Place just off St. James's Street. Alex and I went there for breakfast. It is an elegant building behind the Ritz Hotel and overlooking Green Park. When my year's perk was up I remained a member by subscription and have had reason to be thankful that I did so. The club and its reciprocal establishments in other places were to play a big part in the rest of my life.

The details of that day are not now very clear but eventually we arrived by taxi at Tilbury Dock. Alex came on the ship with me. He saw me to my cabin and met my cabin-mate, Mary Hodges who was going to Uganda to teach history in an African secondary school. Alex and I sat by the empty swimming-pool which looked a bit sad and forlorn on this grey December day, two days before Christmas. We made desultory conversation but I think we were both wishing that the parting was over.

Departure from Tilbury Dock

At last our visitors were instructed to go ashore as the ship was ready to leave. It did not rise to a live orchestra but from somewhere in the depths the tune 'Anchors Away' boomed out and we glided ever so slowly up the long straight dock. Alex was the last to leave the quay. He stood resolutely on the furthest point waving a white handkerchief until for me he became a tiny blur, partly because of the growing distance and partly because the tears had come for the first time. As we headed for the open sea and Alex completely disappeared I had a strange feeling of unreality and felt a strong need to hold on to something. In those first moments of departure Mary Hodges and I turned to each other. We were about the same age and our companionship grew and lasted. Soon we were sharing our lives up to that point, both very conscious that this ending was a new beginning. For Mary there was an additional factor. She had just moved from Anglicanism to Roman Catholicism. Her Ugandan school was run by nuns. We had so many interesting things to explore in each other and we had three and a half leisurely weeks in which to do it.

How I appreciated this sea-voyage! It provided space, a blessed hiatus and rest. All the busyness of the last few weeks fell away. Nothing more could be done about what was left behind and nothing yet about what was to come. To an extent this is true of all travel but somehow on shipboard where a collectivity of people quickly becomes a community, the experience is special. We were temporarily cocooned. Young, philosophical and energetic, Mary and I quickly recovered from the leave-taking, adapted to this situation, and began to enjoy ourselves.

Part 2

The Ugandan Years

1960 – 1965

'All this and Heaven too'

attributed to Matthew Henry 1662-1714

Aboard the S.S. Kenya Castle - bound for East Africa, January 1961

Chapter 9

Journey to Kampala

Cabin 182c

In my Quiet Time drawer I have a small book, 'Daily Light'. Just inside it is a card with a picture of the Virgin and child. Written on the card is 'Christmas on board SS Kenya Castle. Best wishes and prayers for the future from Mary - Cabin 182c.' The book was a parting present from Jean Gray. It has been much used over the years; the card which I placed in it on that first of my exotic Christmases is a constant reminder that those wishes and prayers were effective.

The first few days aboard, as the ship made its way southwards towards the Bristol Channel and then to Gibraltar, our first port of call, was a time of setting up 'house', of becoming familiar with the ship and its routine and of meeting our fellow travellers. For Mary and me at least this was an almost dreamlike experience, especially as it incorporated the festive season; for many others around us, travel by ship was nothing new. They were hardened colonials. Some of them even played bridge for most of the voyage and hardly appeared on deck at all. They had seen and done it all before, possibly even to celebrating Christmas and New Year at sea.

Mary and I were grateful, however, for the guidance and advice of lots of people we met, relating not only to life on the ocean wave but also to the future in East Africa. We even had some coaching in the Swahili language while we continued to enjoy the voyage and all the amenities of a five-star hotel afloat. With only about four hundred people on board, there was plenty of space and time to be leisured. And it seemed to me that the staff worked hard to make life easy and pleasurable for us. This was an experience very different from the cruising of modern times, some of which is rather like a Butlin's holiday camp at sea. The passenger liner, now virtually a thing of the past, was a necessary means to an end before air travel took over. The facilities for fun and games were there if you wanted them but many preferred to be restful and to do their own thing. And that was possible.

For Mary and me, Cabin 182c soon became home. We had quickly unpacked and stowed away our things, laying out on the tops of the chests of drawers, our departure presents and telegrams and even flowers. Our stewardess found us vases. And later we began a travelogue, mounting postcards and a map on the wall. Mary had brought a small Christmas tree so we prepared for the big day in forty eight hours time. It just seemed so unbelievable. Each cabin had a steward and a stewardess, red bell for the former, green for the latter. We soon made friends and did our best to keep the place tidy for them as the captain, ex-Royal Navy, was apparently very strict and did an inspection every day. This was good for all of us. The cabin was L-shaped with the double bunks (me on top) in the shorter part, and the wash-basin and porthole at the end of the longer. In rough weather our luggage tended to travel up and down the long bit hitting the walls with regular thuds! But I cannot remember being greatly disturbed. I slept like a log most of the time, and I am happy to say that neither Mary nor I were ever seasick.

From our new home we ventured out, exploring the several lounges, promenading the decks, eleven times round being the measured mile, and of course enjoying the wonderful food. The meals were the highlight of our days. As soon as one was over we looked forward to the next. I gained a stone in weight over the voyage! We had also to become acquainted with safety precautions and boat drill and with practical amenities such as the laundry and ironing rooms and the hold which contained luggage we might need and could be made accessible. These were all in the bowels of the ship as were the hair-dressing salons and bathrooms. You asked the bath-steward to run a bath for you. This was fun in rough weather. It appeared to me that when the ship rolled I went one way and the water the other! As we entered the Bay of Biscay the rolling and pitching increased and even some of the stewards were sick. I think my experience of sailing in Scottish waters had hardened me to storms and I was pleased to be able to hold my head up now. But we did have a few calm, sunny days even in the Bay of Biscay when it was possible to sit on deck, well-wrapped up.

Christmas at Sea

The service on Christmas morning taken by a clergyman passenger in one of the lounges was perhaps less well attended than it might have been because of the weather and also maybe because of the late night dance the previous evening. Christmas began for us then. There were functions of some kind every evening, films, tombola, dancing. We even had music recitals as there was a concert pianist on board. But the Christmas dance was special. It was lovely to see the officers in their formal dress uniforms and it was so exciting to dress up ourselves. I had all my grand new dresses and accessories. I could be leisured about selecting what to wear and taking pains to look my best, something I have to confess I had had very little time for in the past.

The ship was beautifully decorated with large Christmas trees at strategic points. The children, of whom there were about ninety, had a party of their own and Father Christmas piped aboard. Flags with F and C on them were flown from the mast. There was a superb Christmas dinner and all the trimmings after which most needed a siesta! But the celebrations went on privately during the rest of Christmas day. It was a memorable time. I managed to send a greetings telegram home from the radio office. That was quite thrilling.

Gibraltar and Genoa

It became calmer and warmer as we sailed down the length of Portugal. And when we reached Gibraltar it seemed that summer had come. We arrived at 7.00 a.m. There were the twinkling lights of the bay visible from the porthole when I woke up and all around us the busy noises of a ship in port. The arrival and departure procedures at all our ports of call drew me to the deck. I never lost interest. There was the work of the pilot. Various flags were raised, Blue Peter, Immigration and Quarantine. There was the berthing and the lowering of the gangway and appropriate officials coming aboard to interview the purser. Then the different ports had their special concerns. For example in Port said, our health record was of less interest than the passenger list. If we had been carrying Israelis we would have been in trouble. So far as we passengers were concerned, as soon as we left one port, all the information needed for the next appeared on the notice-board, details of tours, postage rates, currency and instructions for those disembarking. It was all very well organised. Here in Gibraltar a tender conveyed us to the quay. Mary and I went on a tour by taxi through the narrow winding streets. We saw the famous barbary apes and the relics of the many wars in which this strategic place had been involved over the centuries. Our driver lamented the ending of the most recent one as business for him had deteriorated since the navy had left!

At the Spanish frontier, British army and helmeted police officers kept a wary eye, as they stood under the Union Jack and watched various Spaniards coming through the barrier. Gibraltar seemed very Spanish although it had been part of Britain for so long. But politics were far from our minds as we enjoyed the luxury of not needing a coat. The sun shone warmly and, for us, strangely on the Christmas decorations.

Back on the ship and making next for Genoa, it was possible now to sit out on the decks and life became very comfortable, except for a little excitement somewhere near the Balearic Islands when the engine suddenly stopped and black smoke began to pour from the funnel so that we could no longer see the sea. We felt very lost and isolated. We learned later, by which time all was well, that something had gone wrong with the feed to one of the boilers and the wrong kind of water had been going in. They had had to stop the engine and do a cleaning job. Hence the black smoke. When it cleared we were cheered by our first glimpse of Africa, of the high mountains behind Tangier.

Another little worry, for those of us going to Uganda at least, was the news received at this time that troops had been sent to quell some kind of up-rising there. However, those who were returning and knew the country well reassured us. It would be merely a precautionary measure and the whole business would be over before we arrived. Which it was.

The sun really shone for us in Genoa. The sky was cloudless and very blue. We were in this large, busy port for the best part of two days. It was interesting to see the old medieval architecture and all the memorabilia of Columbus' time. An outstanding feature of our visit was the tour of the famous cemetery. The cloistered mausoleum is well worth seeing. There was a shop on the ship but its stock was limited and it was good to do a little shopping here. I remember buying a cake which reminded me of Scottish black bun, a speciality of Hogmanay (New

Year's Eve). It was the evening of December 31 st. when we left Genoa, the last day of the year and our last European port. When next we touched land we would be in Africa.

Throughout all these interesting experiences I had to keep reminding myself that I was not just on a short holiday and going home soon to share my story with my family. It would be a long time before I saw them again. I had started a five-year diary on the day I left home but the space for each day was very small. It was now on the ship that I began my serial letter which continued all the time I was in Uganda, and indeed throughout my life. It was not only a means of communication with home. It became for me a kind of therapy and catharsis in the manner of a journal. The habit of keeping a journal has never left me and all through many years of travel I have written on the hoof as it were and often as things were happening. I remember a Japanese gentleman in an airport lounge asking me if I were writing a book and being somewhat startled to be told - yes - and that he was in it!

So I spent much time on this voyage, sitting at a writing-desk in one of the lounges, 'talking' to my family. I even had replies at later ports of call. It was exciting to see the envelope which had been pushed under the cabin door! When my mother died in 1984 I found that she had kept all my letters, ordered by date, thus facilitating this account.

New Year Celebrations

I had let slip to other Scots aboard that I knew something about Scottish dancing. I was persuaded to run a class and given the use of a room and music centre by the purser, on condition that we demonstrate and lead some items at the New Year's Eve dance. The class had begun while we were still in stormy waters and the first few sessions often ended hilariously with the 'sets' ending up in a heap on the ship's rail. But we pressed on and were able to fulfil our obligation at the dance, not only that but to draw in others, and the dancing sessions continued until we were overcome by the heat. The New Year function was a grand affair, some of us lending a touch of tartan to the finery. We were even visited by Old Father Time.

But New Year's Eve was a Saturday and our strict captain insisted that the fun and games should end at midnight. Officially they did but the Scots had ideas of their own and there were private parties all over the place with first-footing of cabins. I had an American and an Irishman I remember, both tall, dark and handsome, who crossed my threshold ahead of me. Mary was visiting elsewhere. The men watched me open my parcel which the family had given me for this night. It contained a piece of coal for good luck, some shortbread and a 'bottle'. They shared the latter with me. Much later I found myself doing a highland fling in one of the bars, the first time I had been in any of them! We had to be fairly quiet as the captain's quarters were above. But in fact when I got to know him later I realised that he had a grand sense of humour and would probably have joined us.

We were fortunate to see Stromboli in eruption as we passed down the coast of Italy. This was spectacular and awe-inspiring. And soon we were through the narrow Straits of Messina and heading for Port Said. We were now in the heat of the eastern Mediterranean. The swimming-pool was busy and all the deck games in full flow. I was on the Entertainment Committee and had a busy time helping to organise and chase people up for matches. The officers were now in their white uniform and sometimes we danced in the open air with the moon smiling down upon us. How rich are my memories of these wonderful nights at sea!

An Arabian 'Night'

Very early on the 4 th. of January we reached Port Said. The night-watchman knocked at 5.30 am to tell us that our safari was ready. It was an exciting awakening and the start of a real marathon. Children and the elderly had not been encouraged to go. We went ashore by means of a pontoon jetty which lurched and shook rather ominously, and all around were the vendors shouting their wares, dozens of little boats with men selling all manner of articles from model camels to riding-whips containing daggers. Palm trees bordered the water-front, behind which were small shops or dukas, and large yellow buildings with flat roofs and wooden balconies lined the roadway.

At the customs post we had to hand over our passports which would be returned at Port Suez where we were to re-embark. I felt very loath to do this. It was a kind of naked feeling. I also sensed a wariness in the almost surly attitude of the officials. This was only a short time after the Suez debacle and Britain was not much loved just then. We were to see great new factories shooting up everywhere, built with money from the Communist bloc!

Three comfortable, air-conditioned coaches took our party to Cairo. For some distance we followed the Suez Canal, and watched ship after ship joining the south-bound convoy. They came from all over the world, large liners and tankers. One of the costs of this trip was that I never actually went through the canal. We were to rejoin our ship once it was out of it. The road here was no more than a muddy track with military checkpoints at frequent intervals. The country became more and more barren, until we finally turned away from the canal and found ourselves surrounded by miles and miles of desert, a dirty grey sand dotted with outcrops of rock and sparse-looking scrub. It was a bleak landscape. But the road surface improved eventually. To our left was a subsidiary canal and some irrigation channels. I was impressed with a scene of the old and the new together. On one side it was like Biblical times. Camel caravans and donkeys could be seen on the horizon, and ancient shaduffs for collecting water. On the other was the railway and the diesel train.

As we tore along the very straight road, our horn going all the time, people and bicycles scattered and we missed other vehicles by inches. It was hair-raising. We stopped at a rest-house for a drink and then went on again until we finally reached the outskirts of Cairo about 11.30a.m. I found it dirty and noisy and decided I would not want to live there. It had an almost sinister aspect I felt and determined to stick closely to my party. It would have been the easiest possible place to disappear in, and at that time it was well-known as a hive of international intrigue.

Before lunch we were taken to the famous Museum of Antiquities, where we were conducted through a maze of mummies and cases containing furnishings from the tombs. Mary, the historian, would have liked much more time to linger but this was 'the quick trip to Cairo' and we had to cover many things in a short time. After a somewhat indifferent lunch in a restaurant we visited the Citadel and beautiful mosque where thousands of lights which used to be candles lit up the magnificent domes and multicoloured windows and cast a strange glow on the alabaster pillars.

Camel ride to Giza, excursion from the ship

The Muslim call to prayer sounded from the high tower above us. From the ramparts of the Citadel we looked down on the city and we also caught our first glimpse of the Pyramids.

The coach then took us to Giza, a dusty sandy area with camels, horses and donkeys ready to convey us. We could choose our means of transport. Mary and I both decided that we must try the camel. Mine was led by an elderly arab in a striped gown who did not seem particularly friendly. Nor did my mount, chattering rudely with 'camalese' grunts as I hung on for dear life. The ponderous beast raised its hind quarters first and then its head and then ambled up the steep, winding road lined with women and children calling out for baksheesh in spite of numerous notices against this. I felt very insecure and more sea-sick than I ever felt on the ship. On our arrival at the great pyramid I nearly fell off head-first as my steed took a nose-dive. I hate to think of the inelegant display I presented as I finally rolled on to firm ground. Then came the claustrophobic climb inside the pyramid to a small room about half-way to the cone, containing a large open tomb. There was not much to see and none of us stayed long. I found the going down backwards worse than the climb and was relieved to be outside again.

Our camel drivers were waiting to escort us to the Sphinx but Mary and I had had enough of this form of transport and now opted for a horse and cart. We were grateful to our coach guide who was able to soothe ruffled feathers. The cart gave us a very bumpy ride. At the Sphinx we went round the temple at its base and were shown the embalming rooms. Men with lighted candles led us into darkened passages and chambers. It was weird and not a little frightening and we were thankful to be in the sunshine once more. The coaches had caught us up and we were taken to a pleasant hotel for tea, after which we returned to the city centre in the darkening gloom of evening. The noise of klaxons was deafening mixed with the shouts of the street vendors. We stopped in a bazaar and were soon surrounded by traders. Up the back-streets the lights were almost non-existent except for occasional naphtha flares. Men smoking hookahs squatted in doorways as we passed, staring dully after us.

Back in the coach we were taken to yet another restaurant for dinner and then on to Port Suez, about a hundred miles across the desert. I wrapped myself in my tartan stole as it suddenly became very cold. The area was so flat that the lights of the waterfront and the ships in the Canal could be seen for miles. We waited in a hotel, vendors still pursuing us, until the signal came to go to the quay. Our passports were withheld till the very last moment. It was a relief to have them back. Soon we were on a tender, tossing wildly as bigger boats passed. We had two and a half hours to wait in this open boat on the Red Sea, until our ship emerged from the Canal. There was no-one to tell us what was happening as the boatman couldn't or wouldn't speak English. There were stories amongst us about the ship not being able to stop and that we would have to catch a rope-ladder and scramble up the side of the moving ship! I fell asleep and was wakened by Mary nudging me and saying that our ship was here at last. She was a large shadow some distance away. She had been delayed apparently by a huge northbound convoy which had taken a long time to clear, and it was nearly 3.00 a.m. when she appeared, anchored and lowered a Jacob's ladder. Fortunately this was substantial and the ship was stationary. We pulled alongside and, cold and stiff, climbed aboard helped by the ship's officers. A hot meal was ready for us in the dining-room. We had come home, and so our Arabian night was over.

Red Sea Frolics

It was difficult to believe that we had only one more port of call before we reached Mombasa. I almost dreaded that final arrival, so thirled (Scottish and difficult to translate!) had I become to shipboard life and the Kenya Castle in particular. I had decided I could get used to it! The few days in the Red Sea gave time for more fun and games however, and even more serious pursuits such as Discussion and Bible Study. But perhaps the most memorable event of the time was the Kenya Derby when I lost quite a bit of money for people who had backed me as a jockey. I was in the 'Maiden Steaks' (sic) and was riding 'Gloom by Bar without Beer.' The 'riding' consisted of cutting one's way along a tape with a pair of very blunt scissors. I was more successful in the fancy-dress parade where Mary and I won the group section. I went as the Loch Ness Monster and Mary as my captor, taking me to the Queen Elizabeth Game Park in Uganda. I also helped to judge the children's fancy-dress and that was where I got to know the captain who shared my task. I had met him only briefly before at his cocktail party.

'Aden-itis'

On the 8th of January we reached Aden, still British, and a duty-free port. Hence the nickname for the 'disease' we caught. The small boats taking returning passengers to the ship were somewhat lower in the water than they had been going. They were laden with typewriters, cameras and all kinds of electrical goods. I became the proud possessor of a Kodak camera, my first which took slides. I was soon putting it into operation. The weather was glorious on that Sunday when we arrived off Aden, a slight breeze tempering the heat and the sun shining on a deep green sea sparkling with white foam. It was good to be alive. We had had our church service at 10.30 and soon after, the coast was sighted. High yellow cliffs towered out of the green sea, and these against a blue sky and white fluffy clouds, made a beautiful blend of colour. We anchored in the harbour at about 12.30 pm amid a horde of arab dhows and other visiting ships. We were about to take on a large consignment of oil and the bunkering apparatus was alongside. As the tenders took us to shore we could see oil vats and large chimneys everywhere.

Aden must be about the driest place in the world. It has only three quarters of an inch of rain in a year. There was not a trace of grass anywhere. After doing our shopping in the picturesque town, five of us hired a taxi and went for a tour. We visited the ancient Tawela water tanks, said to have been built by the Queen of Sheba. We went to the old arab town, start of the caravan route. It was the first time I had seen women wearing the yashmac.. We saw the salt-pans and found the golf-course, a large bunker with nine holes, as someone had described it. Coming back to the boat we passed through beautiful gardens, a veritable oasis in the desert. It was cheering to see how humankind <u>can</u> bring fertility and growth to the most unpromising situation, with a little help from God!

The Equator

The last big fun event of the voyage was the crossing –the-line ceremony which had of course to wait until we were at the right point on the map. I was not a victim. I did not fancy being tipped backwards into the pool, but some passengers, including children, did volunteer. It was announced very seriously that morning by King Neptune himself that he and his court would be coming aboard at 10.30. He finished by saying – 'Neptunus Oceanus Rex'. In due course we were all gathered at the swimming-pool, cameras at the ready. Neptune arrived in full regalia to regal music, with members of his court. The purser was the prosecuting attorney, complete with gown and wig and spectacles on the end of his nose. The unfortunate prisoners were brought in, roped together, led by two policemen who kept whacking them with their truncheons. There was a grim-looking operating table and the doctor all ready for action. The tipping chair was on the side of the pool, with two men about to slap paint all over the victims before tipping them in. Another two clowns were in the water to see they received a proper ducking.

Each prisoner had a different indictment and the punishment to fit the crime. One poor soul was to have his lights removed, and the doctor held up a string of electric light bulbs. Another had a bone taken out and a huge ham bone was thrown over the side. The means of anaesthetic was a hit with a hammer just above the victim's head. They were kind to the children who did not have any operations.

Mombasa and on to Kampala

Soon after we crossed the equator we headed for our final destination. I recall my mounting curiosity and excitement as we drew nearer and nearer to that distant blur and the dockside derricks loomed ever larger. There is something special about the final arrival of a ship whether you are on it or watching it. At last the engines which had brought us safely from England during three momentous weeks, had come to rest and we were tied up at the quay. The Coast Agent came aboard to help the new Government people. Our luggage was soon sorted and we were on the train, making for Kampala. The journey was to take two and a half days. I recall also a feeling of nostalgia for the ship which we were able to see for some time as we travelled inland and upwards. Now we would not be returning at the end of a shore adventure. There was a momentary sadness.

The train also was like a first-class hotel but this time on wheels. Again I shared a 'cabin' with Mary Hodges. It was a sitting-room by day and a bedroom by night. The steward made up the beds while we were at dinner. Everything was so clean and comfortable and the food was excellent. Flowers graced the tables. There was hot and cold water in every cabin. It was a novelty to be served by an African in a long white kansu with red cummerbund and fez, and to be summoned to meals by a musical gong. But the experience of the train itself was more than matched by that of the scenery we passed through and the stations we stopped at, the first of these being Kikuyu, a name redolent with

Mau Mau memories which were still very fresh. And just past the station we saw a vast reservation where many Kikuyu tribespeople had found sanctuary after the troubles.

This railway line through Kenya to Uganda is several hundred miles long in unbelievably splendid countryside. From the hot sticky coast of Mombasa the train climbs steadily by a series of escarpments till it reaches the summit just under a thousand feet above sea-level, and so winding is the track that we crossed the equator several times. We stopped briefly at the station called Equator. On either side of the line the African bush stretched towards distant hills or just to infinity pregnant with unfathomable novelty and possibilities. I was reminded of John Buchan's book, 'A Lodge in the Wilderness'. I had struggled through his imperialist politics only because of his marvellous description of Kenyan scenery which I was determined to see for myself and here I was with it all before me. Shall I ever forget pulling up the blind on my first morning on the train and finding zebra, impala and giraffe running beside us? The train in its narrow gauge never went much more than forty miles per hour and the animals were able to keep up. It was a wonderful welcome to my new life.

We were able to leave the train at Nairobi, Kenya's developing capital, a place with which I was to become much better acquainted. It was good to stretch our legs and to imbibe something of an East African town. Other place names too which we only passed, such as Nakuru and Eldoret and Kaptagat, were to be clothed in the years ahead with my own personal memories. For now they were part of the arrival kaleidoscope which contained also the famous Rift Valley suddenly upon us as we turned a bend, miles of plain edged by high mountains and peppered with oddly shaped outcrops of volcanic rock. I was to see more of this during a wonderful holiday after a spell in hospital. The valley is a geological phenomenon stretching through hundreds of miles of Africa.

At Tororo we left Kenya and entered Uganda. The scenery was very different, more green and lush. As I looked out on the clusters of houses snuggled amongst the palms, little black faces peeping out at us from the banana groves and sugar-cane, I was overcome by a great surge of happiness. I had a strange feeling of coming home. There was the huge Lake Victoria the size of Ireland, and Jinja where the mighty River Nile begins its long journey to the Mediterranean, further tasters of the exotic which for me was to become the norm. As the train approached Kampala my tummy did a little dance of excitement and suddenly we were there. The three and a half weeks of suspended animation were over and my new life began. It was like a dream come true.

Map of Uganda

Chapter 10

The Pearl of Africa

The Uganda Protectorate

The next five years were to become the most momentous and action-packed of my whole life. I reckoned they merited about as much time and space as the first thirty-two in Scotland, so I have devoted this second half of Book 1 to my life in Uganda. And once again the main time-line has its places of pause for elaboration and particular stories. My Ugandan sojourn could well have been a book in itself.

Not only were these years significant and exciting for me personally, but they were also so for the country. The Uganda Protectorate became independent from Britain in 1962, almost half way into my stay and just as my first tour was ending. I was caught up in the vortex of change which was affecting all the countries of the empire in the early sixties. Although it had not been made clear at my interview, I was supposed to be training a Ugandan to do my work. The word, 'Africanisation' had been coined linked to the Swahili word, 'Uhuru', meaning 'freedom'. Had I been more politically aware before I left home, events in neighbouring Kenya, especially the Mau Mau rebellion of the Kikuyu tribe in the fifties, and various up-risings in the Belgian Congo following independence there, might have given me pause for thought and stopped me from going to Uganda. How very thankful I am that they did not! I should have deprived myself of an experience whose fulness is difficult to put into words and one which was to be seminal in my life story. In living through these years of extraordinary happenings in Uganda I came to love the country and its people and to pray that God's will would be done in their land. It was a time of tremendous anticipation and high hopes.

A Country of Richness

Sir Winston Churchill in his journalistic wanderings early in the 20th century, called Uganda, 'The Pearl of Africa'. How right he was! Climatically, for instance, it is a delightful place to be. Straddling the

Equator it should be unbearably hot but most of the country, a vast plateau ringed by hills, is about four thousand feet above sea-level. The result is like a good summer in a temperate zone, all the time. There are no seasons of summer, winter etc. only times when the rain which falls frequently, becomes heavier and more frequent. People speak of the big rains (March-May) and the slightly less big (November). Around Lake Victoria in particular there can be some quite frightening thunderstorms and periods of high humidity but there is nothing like the discomfort in this respect to be felt at the coast.

Scenically too Uganda has a great deal to recommend it. It is hard to beat for the beauty and variety of its terrain, from the lush growth areas of Buganda to the arid deserts of Karamoja, with a flora and fauna equally impressive and diverse, even to the primeval plant-life of the Rwenzori foothills in the south-west. These Mountains of the Moon as they have been traditionally called, offer the wondrous sight in an equatorial land, of a glacier on their lofty summit, to be glimpsed by the naked eye from the plains below when the sky is clear. The phenomena of nature in the pearl of Africa know no bounds.

By 1960 much of all this richness had been conserved in national parks which I was privileged to visit, where at that time the wild life roamed in great profusion and where a notice like, 'Elephants have right of way' was commonplace. But all over the country the impact of nature – hills, forests, water in lakes and rivers with falls roaring and tumbling over towering rocks – seemed to be the daily accompaniment to life. Even in Kampala, which at that time was a small but growing town whose boundary touched the bush, I never felt far away from this natural grandeur, with leopards at the bottom of my garden! Everything was writ large.

Uganda had much to offer also in terms of resources. Things seemed to grow while you watched. Coffee was the main crop but there was also cotton, tea, tobacco, sugar and umpteen kinds of vegetable and fruit, particularly the banana. Besides the small sweet variety of this, the large plantain was grown. The banana shamba or plantation which provided these plantains, was much treasured. It was the source of matoke, a staple food. One got the impression of a veritable land of plenty where no-one need starve. And there was also mineral wealth such as copper, tin, limestone and phosphates.

Uganda was a paradise for humankind to live in, did they but use it right, and thereby hangs a tale which I can tell only in small part, the part of the pearl which I experienced, and a little of the stories of others, from the events following my departure in 1965. A return visit in 2002 was a traumatic experience for me but I am happy to say, before going any further with my tale, that out of the mixed emotions which that visit evoked, I came away on a tide of thankfulness and hope. The pearl of Africa which had been greatly tarnished over years of misrule, has begun to sparkle once more.

Impressions in the Sixties

I am writing neither a history nor a political treatise. These topics are more than adequately covered elsewhere. But in order to give my own story some context I must offer something of the political situation as I saw it in the sixties. Uganda was a protectorate and not a colony as was Kenya for instance. No European could own land in Uganda so there were no white settlers. The Europeans were there to rule, administer and protect, though I had some difficulty understanding from what exactly! I later found a few answers in the history books.

The early explorers of the 19th century, men such as Speke who discovered the source of the Nile, found also a well-established kingdom on the shore of Lake Victoria (christened by the British!) with a king or kabaka who was a powerful potentate. That land was Buganda. Missionaries followed the explorers, both Christian and Muslim and people of other nations besides the British. As this area of Africa began to 'open up' to European and arab nations and the kabaka sold his own people for guns, (the slave-trade is a blot on everyone's escutcheon), the incomers assessed the potential for *their* countries and the possibilities of expansion and profit. The squabbles of the outside powers over the allotment of the land and the squaring off of territory in arbitrary fashion whether or not the native tribes were divided, is a tale which makes for sorry telling.

By the early 1890s the Kabaka of Buganda had reached the end of his tether and was tired of being 'got at' by so many different people each pushing a particular interest on behalf of a distant nation. To be brief, and I ask the reader's indulgence for this somewhat simplistic narration, an agreement was made with Britain in 1894 in which 'protection' from the other 'predators' was offered and accepted. And so the Protectorate of Uganda was born. The country that emerged and to which I was appointed as a colonial civil servant in 1960, was roughly the size of Britain. It consisted of four main native kingdoms of which Buganda was the most influential, and a number of other 'bits and pieces', the whole divided into regions and districts administered by British Commissioners. The kingdoms were given a fair degree of autonomy but the British government had jurisdiction over the 'big' departments such as Justice, Defence, Education and other national amenities.

The seat of government was established in Entebbe, a pleasant place on the shore of Lake Victoria, cooled by the surrounding forests. A railway was built from the coast at Mombasa to Kampala which greatly helped to change the scenario. Not only did it bring ease of transport of goods and people but it drew into east Africa large numbers from the sub-continent of India, some to work on the railway and others to establish businesses along its route. Uganda gained a fair proportion of these people who were to become 'settlers' in a way that the British never did. The Wahindi or 'duka walahs' became a firm part of the Uganda scene, particularly when the power base moved from Entebbe to Kampala. In this new capital and indeed in all the other towns which grew in the country, the people of Indian origin established businesses which they ran astutely and well. By the time I arrived in 1960 they numbered about 50,000 and were a vital part of the infrastructure. They were also known as Asians rather than Wahindi or Indians, presumably since the partition of India in 1947, because some of them would come from the area now called Pakistan.

And so in the Protectorate of Uganda there were three 'layers' of population. On top were the Europeans which meant 'British – Whites – rulers' (so an American or any Caucasian was a 'European'), in the middle were the Asians or shopkeepers and at the bottom the Africans who were servants to the other two. There was quite a marked apartheid, particularly in matters of housing and education. To give them their due, the administrators recognised that differences of culture and custom had to be catered for and this can be difficult without some kind of departmentalisation. Sadly, however, it can lead to institutional racism in the top layer, some unease and even fear in the middle and a growing resentment and bitterness at the bottom. Uganda would live to rue this day.

Meantime I, an innocent abroad and full of a sense of adventure, arrived in Kampala to begin my life as an Education Officer within this framework. So little had I known about Uganda that I had been surprised to find Asians there and to be offered a post in Shimoni Teacher Training College which was exclusively Asian. But I soon accepted and began to enjoy the experience. Looking back now I can see that we Europeans were a bit like Nero, fiddling while Rome burned. There was a kind of laissez faire of the rightness of everything. In tidy and orderly manner the rich man was in his palace and the poor man at his gate and the impression given to a newcomer like myself was of a benign ruling power, a kind of Pax Britannica in which each in his place was being protected and cared for in a regime that would never end. And with this regime went all the pomp and circumstance of the Victorian era. The plumed pith helmets of the Governor and his retinue at official events sent a thrill up my spine. I was a 'child' of my place and time. The questions would come later. However I remember one early piece of rebellion when I refused to sign the Governor's 'book'. When your name was there you would be invited to the garden-party etc. I did not want to wear a posh hat and gloves!

But I count myself fortunate to have lived and worked in the Uganda of that time. Though based in Kampala I had many opportunities both within and outside my official 'curriculum' (as I used this word in Part 1, to mean my expected duties) to enjoy the wonders of the country. I share *some* of these as my story continues. Would that I could spend time on my wonderful excursions to Murchison Falls, the Queen Elizabeth Game Park and, on one occasion, to West Nile, where I helped a nursing friend with her work in a mother and baby clinic which she had set up, miles from anywhere. Leaves took me also beyond Uganda's borders. I even went to the Kariba Dam and the Victoria Falls. My own personal dreams and pleasure though were enjoyed amid the flux of political ferment, and in the down-to-earth situation of living and working in this strange unequal multiracial world, the outcome of the fraught history which had resulted in the Uganda Protectorate. The enjoyment of my white privileges and the whole exotic wonder of my new life were tempered gradually by concerns of ethics and justice. I began to question many of the things which seemed to be taken for granted. I followed critically the political processes which were leading to self-government and then to full independence.

Tours 1 and 2

On my first tour I worked happily within Asian Education, getting to know that community and rejoicing in the diversity of Indian faith and culture. I had many delightful students, though as time went on I became very concerned for the girls. It seemed to me that this education as teachers was a kind of bride-price and that girls were given a glimpse of freedom, which they would never really attain. Most of my colleagues were European, but there were one or two Asians and this number gradually increased. We worked extremely well together. At the same time I was acquiring a growing number of European friends outside college, with whom I shared worship and leisure activities, also the strange 'problem' of living in the last days of the 'Raj'. But perhaps the strangest thing of all for me was having a servant, or houseboy as he was known. I had never experienced a servant of any kind, let alone an African man, amongst whose jobs it was to waken me in the morning with tea and to wash my linen! How to handle this situation took some thinking about. As one of my grandmothers *was* a servant my genes were not best equipping me for playing the grand lady! I laugh when I remember discussing 'the servant problem' with friends, in the manner of the Victorians.

My second tour took me to the Makerere University College. There I had students from the 'cream' of all the Uganda communities. I also had academic African colleagues for the first time, and I found myself with more and more friends from every 'layer' of society. The country was by that time independent and to my joy there seemed to be a gradual merging of the races. Would that it could have continued. The next chapter and a little of chapter 13 records my Shimoni experience and includes the build-up to Independence Day on 9th October 1962, and then follows a change of place and pace where I attempt to give the essence of my life at Makerere in the post-Independence-Day period. Sadly the seeds of trouble ahead were already beginning to show and the pearl of Africa had started to lose its sparkle.

Chapter 11

Education Officer

Kitante Court

On arrival in Kampala in January 1961 I was met at the station by Guy Branthwaite and his wife. Guy was Principal of Shimoni Teacher Training College to which as an Education Officer I had been assigned. A pleasant, easy-going Englishman with whom I was to work well, he was my immediate superior in what I was to discover was a very hierarchical service. Also at the station was a lady called Jean, another colonial civil servant, who looked after my immediate needs and introduced me to Kitante Court, the government quarters for the unattached. Married staff had houses in the European area of the town. After one night in the Imperial Hotel, a luxurious (or so it seemed to me then) establishment in the centre of Kampala, I was eventually re-united with my luggage which had been well looked after by government agents, and found myself in a flatlet in Kitante Court. I felt a bit like a spinning-top which had at last come to rest.

In an incredibly short time my flatlet became home. I was just so thrilled to have a place of my own for the first time in my life. The flatlet was one of sixteen, four up and four down on either side of a central arch in a block fondly known as the horse-boxes! Newcomers were put here until a 'proper' house or flat became vacant. Each flatlet had a small study sitting-room and even smaller balcony bedroom which must have been fairly open to the elements as I remember being rained upon and having to move my bedding into the inner room. The usual offices were at the end of the corridor. We each had our own bathroom. The Public Works Department furnished the place with the basic necessities, including a desk. There were even curtains and some cushions, but these things had to be augmented by personal extras. There was no need for kitchen equipment as there was a 'mess' where meals were served communally. I was tickled by the regimentation and the military nomenclature. My first indication of this had been a warning that I would be 'disciplined' if I did not take my daily paludrine tablet and then got malaria.

Kitante Court, straddling both sides of Kitante Road and fairly near the centre of the town, exemplified the lushness of the Buganda area. I had the feeling of living in a botanic garden full of gorgeous trees and shrubs, amongst which hundreds of beautiful birds swooped and fed and pierced the air with their multilingual cries. The dawn chorus was worthy of a concert in the Albert Hall. And not only birds shared our dwelling-place. I soon discovered the prolific insect world, sometimes painfully! I was warned to be careful of snakes and when after six months I moved into a thatched roofed cottage, I found that one or more lived in my thatch! In the valley which was an extension of the Court on my side of the road, leopards roamed freely. This was the Kampala of the sixties, a conurbation on the edge of the bush which seemed loath to give way to the growing needs of the human race. The primeval wildness was never far distant.

We were a scattered community of white-washed cottages, each with its balcony, the place of the sundowner to which I was quickly initiated. As the tropical twilight made its fast descent we would meet on one balcony or another and share the news of the day over a drink, then make our way to the mess for the evening meal. We joined our fellows coming in all directions along the paths which linked our houses, both paths and dwellings built in arbitrary fashion and giving the impression of a natural village. The mess, with its large comfortable dining-room and upstairs lounge, was the hub of Kitante Court. It was here that we picked up our post, laid out on a table in the porch; it was here that we learnt the latest news on the 'bush telegraph'. I was given my table by Mohamed, the maitre d' and so I was welcomed into the 'charmed circle'.

In addition to the cottages there were two blocks of four flats to which many of us aspired as they were less vulnerable. Before I left the Court I was lucky enough to get one of these. Because, sadly, crime was rife and matters of safety were never far from our minds. But the place was well guarded by security 'police'. These askaris went round in twos and I became used to the regular tramp of feet and the muffled voices in the night watches. There were also large security lights.

Even our trusted servants, it seemed, had to be carefully watched. I had soon acquired Lousiano who came to me highly recommended by his previous mistress who was leaving the country. But worrying stories did circulate. Some said that Mohamed in the mess was a kind of mafia godfather. In his supervision of our meals, dressed in smart white kanzu with red cummerbund and fez, he was always the suave, genial servant. The other waiters were similarly dressed but Mohamed had an extra crossband to indicate his rank. He knew all the comings and goings of his clients and also those of their personal servants. It is not so difficult to believe that some kind of nefarious network was in operation. The political climate was right for such things and where better for spying out the land than a community of civil servants representing all departments of the ruling government? I, along with many of my friends, suffered from crime of one kind or another, either political or simple, straightforward burglary.

But in those early days of my stay, these matters were far from my mind. I had my lovely new home, my servant and a growing number of friends all anxious to introduce me to the ways and 'delights of the club'. Kitante Court was the ideal place for me to be, because, like Mohamed, I learned much about the running of Uganda from Paddy and Peter; from Enid, Clare, Margaret and many others, all working in different departments, some of them teaching in the European primary school. There was only one, and there was no European secondary school. Some of the older European children attended the Asian secondary schools but most went to boarding school in either Kenya or Britain. All the African secondary schools were boarding and outside Kampala.

My new friends were knowledgeable too about the café life, the cinemas and the night-spots and also places of interest to visit. They took me to the protestant Namirembe Cathedral and to the catholic Rubaga one, each on its own hill. I learned that Kampala was built on seven hills, as is Rome. We went to Mengo where the Kabaka had his palace and the Lukiko, his place of government. I remember in particular the beautiful garden there and the place of the tombs, carefully guarded and expertly thatched.

I loved Kampala with its mixture of cultures. Turbaned Sikhs rubbed shoulders with the Baganda people in vivid costume, women with babies on their backs and cooking-pots or mattresses on their heads. I never did cease to be amazed at the kind of deportment which allowed them to carry such loads without ever dropping anything. There was the European woman with her shopping-basket going into the one shop which sold vegetables and fruit, apart from the markets, or coming out of the one supermarket, preceded by a boy employed by the store to take your shopping to the car. Those were the days! There were the scavenger boys running along in dirty shirts and shorts, clutching large zinc baths full of rubbish and there were the large, expensive, chauffeur-driven cars with 'M' for 'Minister' on the back, all mixed up with the herd of cows driven by ragged herdsmen with large sticks. The panorama was as colourful and changing as in a kaleidoscope.

My good friends also took me on one or two outings beyond the city, to Entebbe for instance with its lovely botanic garden and Jinja, a textile town on the Nile, where the Owen Falls Dam marked its source and which supplied electricity not only to Uganda but also, at that time, to Kenya. I learned so much from them in the short leisurely time before college started, not only about the environment but also about the protocols of colonialism. I had to get used to being a white with a black servant who was about to teach browns. Soon would come the start of term with all that that involved for me, plus, I still had to take my driving test. The few hurried lessons before I left Britain had not been enough to get me there. This was now urgent. But, thanks to the people of Kitante Court I now felt equipped to make a start on these new challenges and I eventually became a driver and acquired a car, a Morris 1000.

Shimoni Teacher Training College

It stood on a rise at the other end of Kitante Road from where I lived. This was extremely convenient for me as I had only two miles to go to work and it was easy in my carless days to get lifts from friends, especially as the college was very near the town centre where all the government offices were. Shimoni was for Asian students, the only one in the country, so we had many boarders as well as Kampala day students. The two year training course was for those who had passed School Certificate. They could specialise in either primary or junior secondary teaching. Students with university degrees and qualified to teach in senior secondary schools, received their teacher training in the Institute of Education at the Makerere College, along with students of other races. So Shimoni was an Asian enclave, particularly as it had a Demonstration school immediately adjacent and a large primary and junior secondary school just across a field at the back of that, all with Asian pupils. There were many hundreds of Asian young people in the total area and there were many Asian schools scattered about the town, some of them of special religious affiliation such as the Goan schools and those belonging to the Ish-nash-eri community. All these schools served as places of teaching practice for our students and over my time at Shimoni I came to know them well. They augmented my college experience of the Asian people and I began to appreciate their tremendous diversity of faith and culture. The community was a kind of little Asia beyond India, situated in the middle of Africa!

For me and a great many others, both staff and students, Shimoni was a very special place, much more than an area of study where students learned to teach, but a real community, almost a family in which, through many different activities, the hundred and fifty of us became very close, learning in the way of families to love and support. This was remarkable as we were such a varied bunch of people. It became even more remarkable when, after 'Independence', African students were admitted. Was this something of the Pax Britannica at work? Most of the staff when I arrived were European though this changed until at the end of my time there I was the only one left. No, I don't think this was the reason though there may have been something of it. We were fortunate in the two principals who were there in my time, very different in their approach but both running a happy ship. When Guy Branthwaite was leaving and returning to Britain, I was asked if I were interested in taking over. Shades of my St Katherine's days. I refused. Administration was not for me. I was glad that I did so. Ganesh Bagchi, the Headmaster of the Demonstration school, became our next Principal and his gently strong handling of the college through the lead-up to 'Independence' and beyond, will long be remembered in the minds of many. A Bengali, Ganesh is one person in my life (happily still alive and living near me in England) whom I see as truly multicultivated. His knowledge of both

Tagore and Shakespeare for instance is phenomenal and says it all. In those college days this kind of influence had an effect beyond the sum of its parts as one student, an African, still likes to relate. Charles Kabuga was one of the African intake after 1962. He had difficulty finding a place to live as the college hostel was full and the room he found in town was tatty and damp. Ganesh offered him space in his home where he lived with his wife and three children on Kololo hill amongst the Asian community. Charles became one of the family. The children loved him and when the parents went to India on leave he was left in charge. He was also introduced to people of all cultures, people cultivated like Ganesh himself, and he joined house-parties, some of them on the university campus on Makerere hill. With his ability to reach out and accept and understand diversity, Ganesh in his profession was doing far more than teach classroom didactics. I basked in his reflected glory and like to think that I was able to put something of what I learned into practice. It is certainly true that my growing interest in multiculturalism which I have never lost, began at Shimoni.

My original remit in the college had been as lecturer in charge of Infant Methods. The lady doing that work was leaving. As it happened, so was the gentleman in charge of English. Coming so recently from my course in London on Teaching English as a Foreign Language I was keen to put my new ideas into practice. I persuaded Guy to let me do the English work if he could find someone else to do the Infant Methods. He did so and I then became in charge of the English work throughout the college. This was a real challenge. I was given a free hand in drawing up my programme. The syllabus had to balance language and literature work with methods of language teaching. I spent many hours pondering the best use of time, and organising teaching demonstration and practice. It seemed to me that the custom had been simply to follow the course then being used in the schools, showing the students how best to use it. This of course was important but I was not all that impressed with the course and I felt also that the students should be given a wider vista of the English language. So I based my syllabus on the skills of listening and speaking, reading and writing, with a fair degree of emphasis on the first two, which at that time was an innovation. Now suddenly several things came together and my role as an Education Officer took on many new dimensions.

My Growing Role

First, I discovered that Ganesh was a playwright. Here he and I really met up. He wrote and acted and I directed. We entered drama festivals and usually did very well. Drama became an important new subject on the timetable and we took part in student festivals. I devised a course in speech training which fitted in well with that on listening and speaking skills. This work at Shimoni became known in many of the African secondary schools, especially those with mainly European staff, several of them nuns. I found myself being asked to help and advise and sometimes to adjudicate school festivals.

Still with drama, I had, early in my time in Kampala, joined the Kampala Amateur Theatrical Society, KATS, and was soon both performing and directing in the lovely new National Theatre. One production followed another till I sometimes began to wonder which was my full-time job. The standard in KATS was very high. Some of the actors had been with professional companies such as the Old Vic in Britain and the expatriate audiences expected professional performances here. They paid professional prices. It was nail-biting, acting in this situation and even more so directing, which I was eventually persuaded to do, but I loved every moment of it. The really wonderful thing about it was that it linked with my college work. The students came to the shows and even to rehearsals. Their speech work and drama improved immensely and so did their teaching. I shall return to the business of performing but first, some other things which came together at this time.

I had begun to attend All Saints, the English-speaking Anglican church on Nakasero Hill. There was no Presbyterian church in Uganda as the denomination had never missionised there. The nearest was in Nairobi, four hundred miles away and the minister came to All Saints Kampala, once a month. I joined the choir so my interest in singing was catered for again. I took part in various activities and attended Evensong in particular, coming to enjoy that service very much and glad that I had been introduced to Anglican ways in my schoolgirl camps in Britain. When the African students joined Shimoni they came to church with me and even one of my Sikh students came out of curiosity and interest. So I found myself sharing not only my professional journey with the young people in my life but also my semi-professional one in the theatre and my spiritual journey. And when I say sharing I am referring to more than the experiences themselves. Very often we had discussions, tutorials in a sense, both in the car as I drove them home and in my house over a coffee. Both car and house became extended classrooms. Even the songs we sang in the car were sometimes useful for teaching English! It was a very special experience for all of us, and more than ever I was conscious of God's power in my life.

But if I had ever doubted this, what I now have to record restored that faith. Early in my Shimoni days and after I had gained some credibility with the Asian community, I was approached by some Hindu gentlemen and asked if I would run a youth club for their boys. Memories of my experiences in North Merchiston and St Katherine's in Scotland inclined me to agree but I made it a condition that I could run a club for girls as well. Somewhat reluctantly this was agreed provided never the twain should meet! Premises in Buganda Road were granted by the municipality and recruiting of members was begun in the Asian secondary schools. At first only boys responded, but they came from all the Asian cultures, even the Roman Catholic Goans. This in itself was exciting and stimulating. I found that I needed help and who better to turn to than my Shimoni students?

The numbers grew and the small building we had been given could not hold us. Also, by this time to my great joy, girls had begun to arrive, not on the same night as the boys, of course! And after a slow start their numbers also began to grow. So I recruited more student help. Soon a sprinkling of African and European young people appeared. What a wonderful extension to the teaching practice this was for my Shimoni folks and what a rich multicultural experience for all of us! But we desperately needed a bigger place to meet, and eventually I approached the Rev. Harries at All Saints Church. Could we use the hall on the church premises? He readily agreed and so it was that the Central Youth Club, as we were known, started to meet in the hall of a Christian church. I well remember our first night there. Just as we were gathering, a number of church members, possibly the Bible Study group, were coming out of church. There were some raised eyebrows when the youngsters, mostly Asian, were seen on the premises. It gave me great pleasure to explain, and to remind my fellow church members that surely this was what

Christianity was all about. How it happened that the boys and girls started to dance together, albeit in fairly neutral and very 'imperial' dances such as the Canadian Barn Dance and the Virginia Reel, I cannot quite remember except that I can still see the boys, on girls' night gazing in wistfully from outside the windows. Somehow this last hour of the girls' evening became a mixed event and a tremendous new fellowship was born. With my Shimoni student helpers there the whole thing began to reflect something which had started at college, the Monday evening social when we sang and danced and shared so much fun together.

It was all very un-Asian. It has been referred to in 'No Place Like Home', An Autobiography, by Yasmin Alibhai-Brown, Virago Press 1997. Yasmin, who became a well-known writer and broadcaster in the U.K., was a girl in my club. If there are any of these Asian parents out there still I have to confess that their boys and girls did come together and also joined with those of other cultures, and perhaps the club – I – was to some extent responsible for the future marriage of Iqbal and Nasma for instance. I cannot think now that what we did was sinful. It was all so warm and full of joy. And somehow we felt that God was not far away. One evening this same Nasma who was fourteen, came to me and asked why we did not have prayer. Somewhat taken aback, though I should not have been, I explained that as she and many others were Muslim etc. and I was Christian, perhaps their parents would not like me to conduct prayer. The girl looked hard at me for a moment and then said, 'But Madam, same God'!

As it says in the Bible, (Isaiah ch.11 v.6), 'A little child shall lead them.' We began to finish our evening with prayer. The children virtually made one up. The name, 'Jesus' was not in it but 'God' was, and I am certain now that Christ was in the operation somewhere. The end of each club night had a special ceremony. We stood in a circle with hands joined as for 'Auld Lang Syne'. Newcomers were asked to stand in the middle. As we sang the Girl Guide song, 'Make new friends but keep the old; one is silver the other gold', we opened the chain and took the strangers in. Then we said our prayer together. Can I ever forget this experience?

And speaking of new members, something else I shall never forget was the recruitment of George Sebagala whom I had been visiting.

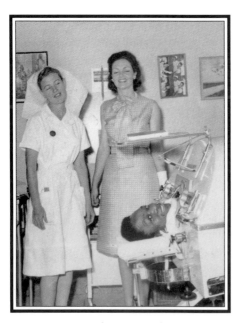

George in iron lung. Visit from wife of Duncan Sandys, the then British commonwealth Secretary.

George was a polio patient in Mulago Hospital, at that time the largest hospital south of the Sahara. He was in an iron lung. I had told him about the club and asked if he would like to join. He was thrilled to do so and we had a wonderful ceremony in his room in the hospital with as many of the club members there as I and others, many my European friends from Kitante Court, could carry in our cars. By that time the club had a badge and George was presented with this. We sang our song and said our prayer and the nurses looked on benevolently. One of my adventures in chapter 14 tells more of George when I was allowed to take him to visit his home. Further memories of the club are many and varied, including picnics and sports days in Entebbe and the hinterland of Mbale, a town in the east from which many of our students came. When they qualified as teachers and went to teach back home or other places, some of those who had helped me in the Kampala club started clubs of their own. This was an exciting development. Another was that we had exchange visits, when Kampala children stayed over in other towns and children from there came to stay with us. By some strange manoeuvring we managed to have Moslems staying with Hindus and Africans with Asians etc. It was an eye-opener for all of us and education of a very special kind. Most of the time we had complete co-operation from both parents and teachers.

And two other matters before I leave the Central Youth Club. I have said that I would speak again about performing, one of my 'things' from childhood onwards. The theatre had given me both drama and singing (I sang as the fairy in the 1961 pantomime!) Now in college and in the Youth Club, dancing was coming to the fore. I felt very much fulfilled in what I was calling my semi-professional journey.

In some quarters I became known as the dancing teacher. My 'fame' had travelled even to the Chinese Embassy. I received a telephone call one day at college to ask if I would come to the embassy to teach the Chinese Ambassador ballroom dancing. The embassy at this time was a very closed and mysterious place behind a high stockade. I was intrigued and accepted with alacrity. But sadly my excited anticipation came to nothing. I heard in a roundabout way that the ambassador's wife had arrived! However I had lots of other dancing 'jobs' including adjudication of festivals in schools, often of Scottish dancing which the Africans especially seemed to love and do very well. My role as an Education Officer was therefore extending further. I also made sure that I took time to learn the dancing of other cultures, both African and Asian. The wearing of a sari reduced my normal stride and forced me to greater elegance.

The other matter concerning the club is funding. Around the time of Independence in 1962 we attracted a grant from the Government. Some enlightened souls saw that perhaps this multicultural way was that in which the 'new' country should be going and it was youth in particular who needed to be educated towards it. I often shed a few tears for what might have been. Sadly came the years of misrule, especially those of Idi Amin when the Asians were sent packing and the infrastructure collapsed. It is interesting to recall that Bob Astles, Amin's notorious white lieutenant, had been very involved in the youth wings of political parties, for whatever reason. I had the doubtful honour of working with him when we both served on a youth leaders' council.

Run-up to Independence and End of my First Tour

As my first tour progressed, the pace quickened both for me and for the country. Politically Uganda was seething with activity as the various parties jostled for support and power and a place in the sun in the new independent Uganda. The date for the Independence ceremony had been fixed for the 9th of October, 1962. My departure date for home leave was to be the 16th of the same month. Because of various happenings, mainly political, my leave came earlier than expected. All around Uganda her neighbours had been involved in independence procedures or were about to be, accompanied by turmoil of various kinds. Our Kabaka had been exiled and returned and a new party called Kabaka Yekka formed, all amid the high-powered discussions going on both in London and locally as the handover drew ever nearer and as some said, too quickly.

Be that as it may, I too had some sorting out to do. I had been head-hunted by the Institute of Education at the university. Makerere needed someone with primary school teacher-training experience to tutor a course which they had agreed to run for UNESCO. The course would be for people to become tutors for training colleges and they would come from a number of African countries. None of the staff at the Institute had the necessary expertise to run such a course. I was honoured by their approach to me. At the same time I had no wish to leave Shimoni where I had found such professional satisfaction and fulfilment, and joy in companionship. Never in my life before or since has there been quite such a work paradise for me. But, reluctantly, I did indicate my interest.

There began now a protracted period of waiting. I was eventually given to understand that the Makerere post was mine if I wanted it but there was nothing in writing. Later I learned that the problem was political. At this delicate moment in the country's history, any new 'white' appointment was looked at askance in certain quarters. Meanwhile my life at Shimoni and Kitante Court went on. I had begun to prepare for my home leave which would last for three months. I had found a gentleman who would live in my flat while I was away and my friend, Teresa, who lived above had agreed to look after the little cat I had acquired if the animal did not take to my tenant. I had to tie up all kinds of ends at home, work, church, club and theatre etc. So many lovely people offered to cover for me. Even my regular visits to George in hospital were taken care of by Helen, a New Zealand friend who had come to teach in the European primary school and who also lived at Kitante Court. I had had to part with Louisiano when he began to indulge in the local and highly potent waragi. His behaviour became very odd to say the least. He was replaced by a somewhat elderly houseboy called Thomas who had known Louisiano well and somehow turned up when he left! Thomas was to serve my tenant and would continue to serve me when I returned. The car, my good friend Paddy would look after. It would be parked at his place. Paddy's wife Sheila and two daughters were to come out to join him soon and he had acquired a house in the European quarter. It was arranged that I would spend my last days there before leaving and Paddy would see me to the airport. However, as our Scottish bard, Robert Burns, says in his poem, 'To a Mouse', 'the best laid schemes o' mice and men gang oft agley', (often go wrong). The lead up to my leave-taking was not to go as smoothly as planned.

It so happened that Miss John, the warden of the girls' hostel at Shimoni, had been given a few weeks' leave of absence to go on a course. She would be back just before *my* leave. Ganesh asked if I would move in as temporary warden to cover for Miss John. Of course I agreed and now my St. Denis school experience came to my aid, though my charges this time were all Asian and grown women. I had in addition to keep an eye on the men's hostel but there was a senior student with some authority there. In normal times this would have been a fairly straightforward job for me, the only really challenging bit being the supervision of the kitchen, never my strong point! However Miss John had left clear instructions to the cook and staff and all should be well. My own coming leave meant that my Kitante Court arrangements had to be put in place just that bit earlier which was not a bad thing as I could cast a distant eye. So, with this eye on my flat and the other on my charges, I moved in to Miss John's room in the girls' hostel much to the consternation of our askari who was used to Miss John's early hours and generally quieter presence! He found that he had to open the gates to let my car in sometimes, as he saw it, in the middle of the night, when I finished some work at the theatre. It was an eventful time in the context of national ferment and some trepidation concerning general security. There was a degree of fearfulness especially amongst Asians and Europeans.

The parents of our girl students needed much reassuring that we would look after them. The girls had to be in their rooms by 9.30 each night. The men had a little more freedom. But on the night of October 8th, the eve of our Independence ceremony, students all over the country were being offered tickets for the rehearsal. Of course ours wanted to go, or some of them did. The others were arranging a farewell party for me that night. So I could not accompany the people going to the rehearsal. I asked a few of our men to escort the girls and to make sure that all got home safely. My party over, I was just about to go to bed when the senior girl student responsible for checking the rooms, came to tell me that a certain girl was not in. My heart sank. This Sikh student had caused a few alarms and excursions as she was being pursued by Dinker Mehta, a Hindu member of the Demonstration School staff. In some ways I suspect she may well have been leading him on. The whole thing had developed into something of a scandal in the college. I had had to confront the burly, bearded and turbaned father with assurances I was far from feeling. Now I could only assume that the girl had taken this opportunity of leaving the college in the evening, to go to her boyfriend in his city flat. I would have to go and look for her. I quickly dressed again and went over to the men's hostel. I dared not risk our askari having a heart attack at having to let me *out* in my car at that hour. I would ask one of the students to take me in his. A Sikh student came to my rescue. He had been preparing for bed and it was the first time I had seen the turban off and the long, flowing hair with a topknot. There was no time for embarrassment. He hastily re-turbaned and we were off, first to Ganesh's house. I felt *he* should be told of what was going on. He insisted on coming with us in spite of feeling groggy after injections for going to India. We went to the boyfriend's flat but there was no-one there at all. There followed a weird excursion which lasted into the early hours of the morning. My memories of it are now a little vague but I do recall us creeping along the balconies of the Asian flats, knocking and enquiring, three somewhat bizarre figures hastily dressed, the Sikh student with his long hair trailing out of his rapidly wound turban. We 'enjoyed', if that is the right word, something of the nightlife of Asian Kampala. It was surprising how many people were still up. Strains of night music pursued our passage and nowhere did there seem to be any curiosity about this incongruous trio, a white woman, a Sikh man and a Hindu man in strange companionship in the middle of the night.

Eventually one of us remembered that our girl had an uncle in the vicinity and after more searching we tracked him down, though we feared the repercussions when Papa was informed. There was no obvious surprise as the uncle opened his door to us at 2.00 a.m. We were ushered in and tea was brought amid all the usual courtesies as though it were two o'clock in the afternoon. At last the purpose of our visit was discussed. To our great relief the student was there. She was sleeping but we asked that she be wakened and brought to us. The worst fears of the night were quickly dispelled. She had drifted from the party at the Kololo Stadium where the festivities were being held and realised she would be late back to college. Rather than risk my wrath she had gone to her relatives instead and it had not occurred to anyone to telephone and let me know where she was. The girl probably slept little during the remainder of that night as she had to look forward to another interview with me and I would not be in the best of tempers!

The next day classes were suspended as the events of Independence Day were enacted. The crested crane which had been adopted as the country's symbol and appeared in the centre of the flag, now decorated our college sign. Once we knew that the British flag had come down we all stood around our sign. Ganesh said some suitable words and we sang the new national anthem which we had been practising for weeks. It was a poignant moment. Why I did not attend the big ceremony where the Duke and Duchess of Kent were representing the Queen, I cannot now recall. Perhaps I was not invited! Perhaps I felt I might just be needed at college in my role as warden. But in some ways it was not necessary to be there as the sounds carried all over the city and the fireworks could be seen from every part of it. We even heard the two national anthems as the British flag was lowered and the Uganda one was raised. Then came the cheering and the sounds of carousel throughout the night. There were to be several days of events. A new Independence arch had been unveiled with a medallion hanging from the centre, of Milton Obote, the Prime Minister. He was the first leader of the independent country, with the Kabaka of Buganda hovering in the background as President. On that joyful day I wonder how many imagined that the seeds of disaster had been planted. In 1966, the Kabaka's kingdom was destroyed by Obote, with Idi Amin as the perpetrator. The Kabaka escaped to England where he died in mysterious circumstances. And so began the bad years in Uganda.

But let me balance this sombre thought with something I found amusing, whether or not it be true. The story goes that as the Ugandan flag was raised, a Scot sitting next to an African, a new Ugandan, congratulated him on his country's newfound independence. The Ugandan responded by saying, 'Thank you, and now we in Uganda will pray that you too may soon gain your independence.' This surely would have rejoiced the hearts of the Scottish National Party. And speaking of Scotland I now have to turn to the tale of my departure for that land which was only a week away. The gods of excitement could not yet let me relax, however. I moved to Paddy's home as planned after Miss John returned to the hostel and on the night before my flight I went to visit some Asian friends in old Kampala. When I came out of the block of flats, my car had gone. I just could not believe the blank space where I knew I had left it. Both my umbrellas were in it too I remember thinking stupidly. I usually had one in the house and one in the car but for some reason they had come together. Luckily there was nothing of value there. When I went to the Central Police station to report the loss of my car I was somewhat dismayed and later amused to find that the officer seemed more concerned that I was 'Miss' and therefore lacking a husband, than that I now lacked my car. I tried to assure him that I was more anxious to find my car than a husband. I never did find either. The vehicle, with so few miles on the clock, I reckoned had been driven off into the Congo or somewhere. It was too new for the usual stripping of sellable parts.

Poor Paddy! He was left with the problem of finding me a second-hand car for my return. I had still to finish paying up the last, I was not in the habit of hire-purchase, but it was the custom in the Colonial Service to have something deducted automatically from your salary every month until this necessary item was paid. Most of us could not afford a car outright when we arrived, and I could not now afford a *new* car. I flew home (a very different type of journey from that on the ship) in the middle of the next night, seen off by friends who may have been drawing breath of some relief. When I think back I did seem to create a degree of turbulence around me. My first tour in Uganda, the Pearl of Africa, was over. To use a favourite word of mine in letters home, 'Phew!' And even the journey had its problems. We were diverted to Paris because of fog in London!

Chapter 12

Intermission

Unwinding

The prolonged journey was useful for the initial unwinding. I needed this before being absorbed once more into the life I had left. I was to find the adjustment not very easy and it must have taken at least a week before I was able to live comfortably with the change of pace. But once I had 'come to' as it were, I soon picked myself up and began to enjoy my leave. The weeks would go by all too quickly and some planning was necessary. Apart from mundane things like visits to the dentist and the optician and urgent shopping, I must take time to share my recent experiences with family and friends and to return to old haunts. I had acquired quite a collection of photographs and slides. Also I needed to talk with people who had helped and trained me, setting the things I had been doing against their teaching. So during the unwinding period I arranged a schedule.

Initial Events and Impressions

Until the beginning of November I simply enjoyed my family and immediate friends. Dad had now retired and had more time for his golf. I accompanied him round the lovely Baberton course, revelling in the beautiful autumn colours and realising how much I had missed the changing seasons but I also realised that the winter cold was beginning to bite. It was near the start of what was to be one of the most severe winters in living memory and my introduction to the electric blanket! Joan and Dorothy were both in business and living at home. Dorothy had found that nursing was not for her. She had acquired a job with the Dental Board and seemed happy. I was able to relate more to both sisters now as adults and we shared all kinds of ploys. Joan, who was by now an accomplished typist, was able to help me by typing papers I was writing. I had brought some work home. A one-off event I particularly enjoyed was taking Dorothy to an Indian restaurant, proud to share with her my new-found knowledge of Indian food. We also went together to the Plaza dance-hall. Joan and Dorothy were both skilled in the latest dances in which they coached me. I later won the staff/student competition in the Twist, at Shimoni!

Alex was still lecturing at Glasgow University. He came over frequently and we renewed our walks in the hills. Sometimes I went to him. It was good to discuss my own possible university future, especially in the atmosphere of Glasgow's venerable pile. Alex now had a car so our chats were also held in places like the shores of Loch Lomond. And at the centre of the home as always, was Mother. She had been my main correspondent and was already beginning to file all my letters. She was a true home-bird but she followed the roamings of us all. A big family change was the leaving of College Church. For several reasons it had seemed right. The minister was going to start an extension church in Muirhouse, a new housing area. The girls followed him there and became happily involved in its many activities. Joan was also to find her husband in this community. For Mother and Dad, growing older, both the distance across Edinburgh and the hectic life of a new church seemed somewhat daunting. They settled for Barclay Church, within walking distance of Merchiston Park and a more settled, established congregation. I worshipped with them there but I also visited Muirhouse and shared something of the new adventures of my sisters. There was for me the sense of an ending. College Church had launched my spiritual journey and I was sad to see its demise in the family life.

Another family change and one I realised was happening in most households, was the increasing influence of the television. It seemed to me that people were beginning to live vicariously. What was on the screen was much more important than anything that could be happening in the immediate environment or in one's personal life. I found this sad and worrying and at times I felt quite resentful, believing that the exciting stories I had to tell were of more interest than those of the soaps. I could see a whole new culture developing and I could not envisage myself being a part of it. I believe this was the start of my love/hate relationship with the media in general.

But because of the constant impact of newspapers, radio and television I was made much more aware of current events. In Uganda world happenings were very much on the back-burner. It was the time of the American frenzy following the launching of the Russian sputnik and tension was high in an effort to keep the balance of power. The Berlin Wall had been raised the previous year. It was the time of the Cuban missile crisis. Ships of Soviet Russia were making for Cuba carrying fearsome nuclear weapons. This was too near the USA for their comfort and President Kennedy was quite prepared to push that fatal button, or so it seemed then. I well remember meeting with my old colleagues at North Murchiston Club on the night when anything could have happened and all of us trying to keep up an appearance of normality bringing each other up-to-date with local and personal events, while the deep fear of the unbelievable churned in our stomachs. God heard our prayers. The ships turned. My leave continued against this background of world events and we danced and sang to the music of the Beatles! I also enjoyed an orgy of Scottish dancing with college friends. Films and theatre shows were frequent events for me. I enjoyed returning to my old haunt, The Gateway Theatre. Whenever and wherever I could I tried to pick up new ideas for my drama work. I was soon renewing my contacts with Edinburgh friends and groups. It was a great joy to be with Mairi again. Ours was the kind of friendship which picks up immediately, even after a long parting. And of course I visited all the family and they came to me. Sadly both Uncle Willie and Auntie Jean were not well at that time. I spent quite a lot of hours in Portobello and I renewed acquaintance with the old people's groups I had helped to entertain, and showed my slides. Cousin Graham worked the projector when I showed them to the Youth Fellowship.

Particular Highlights

Early in November I spent some days in the south. In London my professor of the language course, Bruce Pattison, took me to lunch. I very much enjoyed discussing my English work with him, and came away encouraged and stimulated. It was fun to re-visit London as though I had known the place all my life. I also went to Cropredy, near Bambury, where Eileen who had assisted me on that schoolgirl camp in Malvern, ran a country school and lived in the schoolhouse. We talked as we sat by the log-fire, and I shared with her the realisation of the vision I had had at Malvern.

My next visit was to Dunford House in Midhurst, Sussex. The place was a briefing centre for those going to work in the 'colonies'. I had attended a short course before going to Uganda. Now, as an old-hand, I had been asked to return to share my experiences with those going out, even though Uganda was now independent. It was a fun weekend. I was amused by one gentleman who wondered how so many people could live in the same box!

In the middle of the month I went to Aberdeen. I was to give a talk and show my slides to the St Katherine's people. I had hired a car and bravely my father came with me. It must be remembered that I had not been a driver before I left home. His courage was well and truly put to the test as this was when the snows came. It had been getting colder and colder and we were not really surprised, but the roads were still clear when we left Edinburgh. There were no motorways in those days and we drove through the centres of the towns. We were in Montrose when the first flakes appeared. By the time we reached Stonehaven the world was white and driving conditions treacherous. Somehow we reached Aberdeen, Dad sitting calmly beside me while I negotiated the skids. I had learnt how to cope with African mud and found the skill useful now. In the city's whiteout we found a hotel. Jean was a hospitable hostess in the evening and next day I gave my talk at St Katherine's with Dad as my projectionist. We even managed to go to my former landlady's family near Banchory. Bill was the factor on Crathes Estate. Somehow I crawled along the narrow lanes banked up on each side by snow and Jean and Dad and I were rewarded with typical Aberdeenshire fare in the Birnies' cosy cottage.

Still ploughing through snow, we went on from Aberdeen to Perthshire, visiting Mary and husband Robert Morton at Wolfhill Farm and their relations on other farms, and finally slithering our way to Glenfarg where Mary's mother lived. We gave slide shows all round. It was hard for any of us to imagine the heat of East Africa as we shivered in Scotland's winter. Meantime, Mother had been glued to the media weather forecasts, imagining all kinds of horrors. This is where a mobile phone would have been useful but no such thing existed then. We arrived home safely but I was beginning to rebel against the cold. I just had to go somewhere warmer and I tried to persuade both my parents to go with me. Mother preferred home, no matter what the weather, and when I look back I see that her preference made it easier for the rest of us to wander. It is always good to know that someone is keeping the home fires burning and is ready with the welcome back. It so happened that Dad's brewing firm from which he had just retired, had opened a British-type pub in Nice. This was the carrot I dangled in front of him. Not that either of us were boozers. It would just be interesting to see the place and for Dad to meet old colleagues and dust his memories. The French Riviera was very tempting and, we hoped, would be a bit warmer than Britain. So I put the plans into operation but we were not able to get bookings until after Christmas.

I had one other big outing, again with Dad, before the festive season. This was to Manchester. Peter Wingard, a Ugandan colleague, was now teaching English to foreign students in the university there. I sat in on some of his classes and found the whole experience extremely helpful. With Dad I enjoyed a lunch-hour concert given by Peter and his wife who were both talented musicians, and visited Mother's cousin Mabel, she of the piano and the presents in my childhood. It was a pleasant few days and though cold there was no snow.

It was now ten days till Christmas. Back in Edinburgh I busied myself with shopping, delivering as many presents as I could. I helped at St Denis with their parties and Nativity play. I had bought a book on stage-makeup and enjoyed trying out new ideas. It was still very cold though the snow had gone, only to return. On Christmas Eve, Alex, Joan, Dorothy and I attended a midnight service and next day we had a family Christmas dinner at a restaurant in the High Street called 'The Wee Windaes'. This was after a big present opening at home. It all brought back for me so many happy memories. We watched t.v. all evening on Christmas Day! The rest of the festive season was very quiet, including the New Year. It was just too cold to go first-footing. But I did go to the 'Messiah' in the Usher Hall, something we had done over the years. There was a bad rail crash at Crewe around that time, weather conditions no doubt to blame.

Now it was time for our Nice holiday. I had booked with British European Airways to fly from Edinburgh to London and then on to France.

In the event, we were snowbound in Edinburgh. As was the custom in those heady days of air-travel, BEA gave us first-class rail tickets to London, free accommodation in a hotel there and fixed us up with a French airline next day. It was such fun to introduce Dad to all these exciting things. Alex was quite jealous. He had been the first to take Dad abroad. They had gone to Paris and the Rhine earlier that year. But I was the one to take him on his first flight. As the French Caravelle lifted into the blue sky above the snow-laden clouds of London, I was relieved to see Dad happily reading his Scotsman like any seasoned traveller.

Even Nice had had snow, the first for fifty years. It was strange to see the palm trees growing out of their white roots and it was scary going in a coach up into the maritime alps to visit Vence and other interesting old towns. The driver had never driven in snow before and we were very conscious of the dizzying drop to the valley below. But it *was* warmer and the sun seemed to shine more. It was a wonderful break. We paid several visits to the pub which was called the Thistle Club and received VIP treatment. We enjoyed strolling along the front, sometimes finding it warm enough to sit, and we shopped in the markets and quaint little shops. We even found a café called the Scotch Teashop. Greatly daring we went one night to a casino, courtesy of the hotel, but only watched. Another day we went back to the airport and were enthralled to see a Boeing take off for Africa. I also obtained permission to visit a lycée and learned something of French education, while Dad rested a while. I tended to forget just how energetic I could be. We enjoyed the French cinema and I found that I could follow General de Gaulle in one of his famous speeches. But perhaps the highlight was our trip to San Remo, just across the border into Italy, even if we did spend longer at the customs than in the country. These were the days of very nationalistic borders in Europe.

Further Memories

I hired a car for the second time and in between the highlights I visited Kelso where Anne was now married to George, and the family in Clackmannanshire.

Doris had had a second son and I was brought up-to-date with news of Norma and Alan and family, in Canada. Apart from meeting friends and former colleagues, I was able to see a few people with links in Uganda. Mrs Walker, for instance, was related to people in KATS. She owned the Braid Hills Hotel. I had meals on the house!

A less pleasant memory is the fire in the chimney. We still had that awful range, All-U-Want, which I once again reckoned was nothing we wanted and it certainly proved its malice on the day of the fire. Poor Mother! But for me the good memories dominated. Even the cold, bleak days served a useful purpose. I was able to catch up on my letter-writing and on my writing of academic papers. My recent talks with Bruce Pattison and Peter Wingard had been very useful in this connection. I was beginning also to write children's stories and had made contact with Nelson's, a publisher in Edinburgh. This was all a precursor to my university experience which lay ahead.

End of Leave and Back to the 'Field'

Quite suddenly it was time to depart. My date for leaving was 30th January. On the evening of the 29th we had a family party in the Golf Tavern, a very old hostelry near Barclay Church. Alex came over from Glasgow. He was about to go on one of his overseas expeditions so this was a joint farewell. All the immediate family were there and lots of friends. It was a lovely, happy occasion for me to go out on. We even made a tape for me to take back. I have it yet.

This time I did take off from Edinburgh airport though the ice made it difficult and I was late for my plane in London. I was rushed by jaguar car to Gatwick and then had a very long wait there. But eventually I was airborne again and the Britannia, or whispering giant as we called it, had begun its twelve-hour flight, as it was then, to Entebbe. Once more life was suspended and I had time for reflection. I took with me so much of what I had just left! The loving goodbyes, the loved voices. I had the tape in my bag. So much of me still belonged to Britain, particularly to Scotland. Should I not stay there and stop causing all this heartache? I began to wonder about the whole colonial thing including the missionary enterprise. Who were we to have imposed our ways upon others? Did God have some grand plan for the world in which we were or had been one of his instruments and was I personally a tiny part of that instrument? These were questions whose answers would be a long time in coming, if ever. Meantime I thought over the events and impressions of my leave.

Perhaps one of the most powerful of the latter was the increasing grip of the media. I realised that it would be good to be away from this and I now understood why people coming back from leave had sighed with relief as they turned to their well-used record-players and favourite music. They were back in the safety of the Ugandan cocoon and away from the frenzy of the headlines. Of course this was sheer escapism but from what, the events themselves or the media hype? Uganda had its own headlines and they were likely to become more frenzied. Television would not be long in coming. We would have to take more interest. The whole media business would soon have its grip on Africa too.

Another impression that I brought away with me was born of my two worlds coming together and what I had learnt. I realised how much more I understood of the workings of our government at Westminster, for instance, by having watched the making of one. The developing can throw light on the developed, sometimes giving new life to what is tired and jaded. I had found myself wanting desperately to change things in Britain as I now knew so much better!

Gradually as the hours passed, and maybe somewhere over the Sudan, Scotland and the UK receded and I started to think ahead. What had Independence done in my absence? How was my beloved Shimoni and how could I bear to leave it, as seemed on the cards? Can one get *too* attached?

Could I really do a university job and would my non-graduate status be a problem? I felt I had come such a long way not only academically and professionally but also in the area of multiculturalism. Surely God had a plan for me and perhaps this work in Uganda was just the start of something, that molecule opening up. At the risk of mixing my metaphors I had realised on my leave how much of the experiences of my earlier life had contributed to those in Uganda. They were like nursery slopes to a skier and that strong sense of a guiding hand was very much with me. Little did I realise then that these musings were to be the basis of my future professional life. I eventually summarised them in what I called the Field and the Focus, framework for my philosophy of language teaching and described in my publications for teachers. I was now returning to my present 'field' and the gods of excitement were at me again. I had not realised that Milton Obote, our new Prime Minister, was on the plane. We had a celebrity arrival. By some quirk of timing it was I who was at the top of the steps when the band struck up the National Anthem. I had to stand to attention, melting in the sudden heat with my winter clothes clutched in my arms. But soon I spotted Francis Lobo there to meet me. Uganda claimed me once again.

Chapter 13

Lecturer in Educational Psychology

A Strange Overlap

Amid the warm welcome back on all sides, I was conscious of a change both of pace and orientation. Though it was some time before I heard anything official about my appointment to Makerere I found myself being involved more and more in university happenings. These were not only professional such as staff meetings, but social. Like my friends in Kitante Court, the people who lived on Makerere Hill had their clubs and associations and I was invited to join things. Because of my known interest in theatre I was asked to audition for the Makerere production of T.S.Eliot's 'Murder in the Cathedral' and was given a part. To my astonishment I even discovered my name on a staff list offering advice on educational television! More of this below.

The pace of living was still hectic but in a different way from that before my leave. Then it was very much to do with the excitement of the local politics and the traumatic handing over of government, which inevitably affected us all. Now it was a personal coping with a strange kind of overlap, when for several months my two jobs ran alongside and crossed. There was much to do, but in a plodding kind of way as the steps of my full immersion in the Makerere Institute of Education were exceedingly drawn out.

Africans at Shimoni

I was conscious too of the accelerating speed of Africanisation. Soon after my return, Dr Zake, the Minister for Education in the new government, visited Shimoni and declared himself very happy at the way in which our first African students had been integrated. In fact we all declared ourselves happy. This was a major event and joy of my overlap months. The Africans, mostly men, very quickly became a part of our Shimoni family. There was a little problem at first when the Asian girls stayed away from the Monday social evening fearing that I would ask

Dancing at Shimoni. The African is Charles Kabuga.

them to dance with the Africans. Our Ganesh Bagchi soon let them know what he thought of that and before long they were dancing together on 'neutral' ground. Dances like The Dashing White Sergeant and other Scottish favourites, with the lads wearing tartan sashes and the girls in tartan pinafore dresses, were a big item in our closing concert that term. Pax Britannicca again? Oh, dear! What had I done?

Most of the African students were Christians and several accompanied me to church on a Sunday evening. One was confirmed soon after joining the college. The Sunday evening took on something of a ritual. College supper and church time clashed a little and it was necessary for the lads to leave the table and run to where I was waiting for them in my car. First they had to bang a glass with a spoon which was the recognised procedure if you wished to make a speech. Then they approached the table where the warden sat and asked permission to leave, without making a speech. And then they ran. Occasionally Surinder Singh was there too. This was the interested Sikh who, I believe, eventually became a Christian. How I got them all into my little Triumph Herald I'll never know.

The car was a second-hand replacement which Paddy had acquired for me after my Morris was stolen. Unfortunately it was trouble prone. Paddy did his best to keep me on the road but after numerous minor and some not so minor problems, the big end went and I returned it to the garage which, we decided, had put the clock back before they sold it. One very good thing about my eventual change of job was that I was able to have a new car-loan and I became the proud possessor of a Peugeot 403, a much more sophisticated and powerful car than either of my other two, just in time for the kind of safari my new work would entail.

Sorrows and Joys

During the overlapping months I continued to live at Kitante Court. A large part of me clung to my familiar anchor. My life there combined with my Shimoni work I was loath to relinquish, whilst at the same time I was excited by the challenge which was opening up. It was a time also of sadnesses and joys. From the outside in as it were, there was the assassination of President Kennedy. Uganda had its day of mourning and its share of the fears of the world. Kennedy had been young and full of promise. The youth in particular knew a great sadness. Then, nearer home, one of our Shimoni men threw himself in Lake Victoria and was drowned and Dinker Mehta took his life by drinking nitric acid from the college laboratory, for love of the girl he could not have. For weeks a great cloud seemed to lie over us. And for me, also, I had the grief of seeing very good friends have trouble with their marriage. Both sought my help. It was a difficult time and it affected my health. I spent a week at St Julian's, a peaceful retreat near Limuru in the glorious Kenya highlands where the sparkling air and the care I received brought me back to an even keel.

But set against all this was the pleasure I had in working intensively on that end of term concert along with an exhibition of work. It was good too that my KATS and Central Club activities continued apace. I was gradually handing over the youth work and was happy to see that several of the Shimoni students and staff were prepared to take it on, offering initiatives of their own. I concentrated in my last months on classes for dancing. For KATS I continued with my stage direction. I had produced 'The Gazebo' before my leave. Now I directed 'The Amorous Prawn', both plays which had just come off the professional stage so it was possible for amateurs to present them. I also took part for KATS in an award-winning one-act play which they staged for the national drama festival.

It was about this time too that the Presbyterian church in Nairobi became more prominent in my life. Its Scots minister, Robert Keltie, and wife Nora, had become close friends. Though not exactly round the corner as the trip to Nairobi was a full day or an overnight journey by train, I did go on several occasions, and sometimes spent a weekend. I joined their church-life and family happenings. I also met the delightful Forresters. Dr Forrester had retired and was spending time as assistant here in Nairobi. This friendship I was able to renew in Edinburgh, as by a strange coincidence, they lived opposite the house my parents moved to in 1964.

The Kelties had four delightful children whose company I also enjoyed. We had many a happy outing together. Robin and Nora and I shared a love of all things Scottish. I remember with great pleasure the impromptu ceilidhs, by the log-fire. It could become chilly in the evening in Nairobi at times. The word 'ceilidh' is Gaelic and really means conversation but is used now more generally for a convivial get-together, usually including music. Robin played his bagpipes and then he and I matched recitation for recitation. One weekend, Nora took me and the children to the nearby game park and I saw my first lion. What a thrill that was! The Nairobi manse was to become a loving staging-post for other adventures both in Kenya and beyond.

Then there was the James family. They lived in Kampala. Jim was a leading man in my first KATS production, 'Watch it Sailor'. Their home became a regular Sunday night venue and I shall always be grateful for their friendship and hospitality. I became godmother to Richard and Susan. Though many of my original friends had moved on I was fortunate that several remained, even some from my shipboard days such as Mary Hodges, my cabin companion, and the Bruntons who lived at Lubowa, a sugar plantation. These friends outside Kampala gave me the opportunity to see something of the wider environment and to have practice in driving on the difficult murram (Uganda word for dirt or gravel) roads. I was to be thankful for my bigger car.

New Life Intrudes Further

So my old life continued to be full and very far from static. But suddenly I was presented with the new. I had to begin teaching the UNESCO course at Makerere before I left Shimoni. The students came from the wider Africa, again mostly men. A reasonably small group, we soon got to know each other and I quickly began to realise why I had gone to Moray House rather than the university in my own student days. What I had learned there was much needed now. A great bonus of the overlap was that I was able to bring my Shimoni and UNESCO students together in useful ways. Professionally I think the Makerere people benefited from observing the work in Shimoni and were eventually able to do some practice there, and socially they seemed to enjoy our extra-curricular activities. It was good too for the Shimoni trainees to mix with these mature students.

Becoming an Academic

At last I received the written confirmation of my appointment. I was to be Lecturer in Educational Psychology in the Faculty of Education and have an office in the Institute of Education. 'Shimoni' gave me a wonderful farewell party and a lovely holiday in Mombasa helped to distance me from what I was leaving. I moved from Kitante Court to a staff flat in Quarry House on the campus of the university. The move was somewhat traumatic as I was burgled soon after settling in and then learned that my particular ground-floor apartment had suffered in this way quite often. I lost no time in having bars put on my windows.

It was not easy becoming an academic, especially on the occasion when our notice-board announced that 'Academic dress should be worn', for some function or other. Although I discovered that both my Moray House and my London College of Music qualifications allowed me to wear regalia, I was very sensitive about the whole business and tended to make myself scarce when my colleagues paraded. But the academic work I began to enjoy more and more, not only the reading and preparation for my lectures but the research and writing for journals. I kept up also with the writing of supplementary readers for the Nelson language course. I was being stretched more and more, and I loved it.

As always I had reason to be grateful to colleagues and friends for their advice, support and affirmation. They taught me so much.

A particular learning situation for me was the High Table culture in the halls of residence, so English and so Oxbridge! I did borrow a black gown (the under-graduates wore red ones) from Hannah Stanton, Warden of Mary Stuart Hall for women, whose High Table I had been invited to join. I learned to sip my sherry in the Senior Common-room with the best of them and then to march in to dine. I just could not believe this was me and I wanted to giggle. I really did on one occasion when I was invited to one of the men's halls. It so happened that a new batch of TEA (see below) students had just arrived. They had decided to have a kind of High Table of their own. When the staff entered we were met by the scene of one table on top of another and students on top of that. Neither the Americans nor the majority of the British who came from the new or red brick universities, had much empathy with Oxbridge traditions.

I was soon absorbed in my new work. The UNESCO course was a one-off and of limited duration. I had to take my part in the main work of the faculty. They offered a BA degree course in Education, combined with teacher-training. I was required to lecture in subjects pertaining to the latter. Then there was the one-year course of training given to graduates from other faculties. I helped here with the supervision of their teaching practice and also with their work in English language. I also became involved with the TEA course, Teachers for East Africa. This was a scheme agreed and financed by the governments of the UK and the USA and those of the three East African countries, Uganda, Kenya and Tanzania, the latter two also independent. Graduates of universities in Britain and America were offered three-year contracts to come to East Africa and augment the indigenous teaching force at secondary level. They trained with us at Makerere for one year, along with the local students, and then worked for the other two years in East African schools.

This course brought an interesting new diversity to the student body. When the British and American students joined the local graduates on teaching practice, we could be met with a situation where, in one classroom we watched an African teaching, next door a Scot and across the corridor an American. I found all this exceedingly challenging and was exercised in wrestling with what I considered to be the universals of good teaching in the context of so many different particulars of individuals and cultures. I took my part also in group tutorials, both as professional and personal tutor. Here again the multinational nature of the groups was a delight. One night there were twenty in my flat, perched on cushions and stools when chairs gave out. The serious discussion which had begun as a tutorial, spilled over into the night and became a 'ceilidh'. The students wore their national dress and all were ready to contribute items from their cultures. We danced, sang, recited, ate and drank and laughed a great deal. It really was a league of nations, working I am sure as such a body should!

These students had become my extended family in the same way that my Shimoni students had shared in my various ploys. And the help was mutual. I was there for them if they needed me and they helped me in all kinds of ways. For instance, I had become involved in tutoring children and Savita from Kenya took over from me on several occasions, doing very good work. Life in East Africa offered so many opportunities. These developing, independent nations needed lots of help and understanding and those who would teach in them had to be well-equipped and also adventurous. There were risks as well as opportunities and I was torn between warning of the former whilst at the same time I tried to open a Pandora's box of the latter. The 'in loco parentis' element of my work took on a new significance, especially for those young people in my care who were so far from home.

Political Problems

But there was a growing sense of unease in the country. All was certainly not well at the top. Milton Obote was making himself into a kind of powerful dictator with promise of more to come. He was to get rid of the Kabaka. There was much controversy over an issue which came to be known as 'the lost counties' in which the kingdom of Bunyoro was claiming certain land back from Buganda. It was hard to follow all the politics and rhetoric. The editor of the Uganda Argus, still a European at that time, was kidnapped but thankfully released. Mail was censored and one had to be very careful not to say anything which would ruffle the feathers of this sensitive young nation. People were deported. There was a famous or should I say infamous incident when some silly European young folks organised a British Empire party. They dressed in Union Jack costumes and said and did all kinds of provocative things, including setting fire to some property. This inevitably brought the police on the scene. The 'Tank Hill' party as it was called because of the venue, seemed to hasten the growth of trouble. The youngsters were deported but the beginnings of a police state were now very obvious. For instance, in firms where Europeans still worked, people found that their desks had been searched. We were urged to carry guns. I got as far as a whistle which I had on me at all times and under my pillow at night. But I couldn't help thinking of that caretaker in St Katherine's Club on New Year's Eve when I slept in one of the lounges, suggesting cheerfully that if I heard any strange noises, I should shout and he would lock his door!

There were strange noises quite often and gunshots became more frequent. But I fear that no-one would have ventured out if I had blown my whistle. A few of my friends began to organise escape plans if it became necessary. Amongst this group were Hilda and Winnie, Scottish ladies whom I had known in youth work at home and who, by a strange co-incidence had come on contract to Uganda to organise courses for youth-club leaders. Naturally we had come together and I helped with their courses. My students did too. These ladies were very active in planning an escape convoy for us and others, and our animals. We would go via the Congo in what might have been a very dicey operation. Thankfully things never came to that.

Teaching Practice in Difficult Circumstances

In this context, teaching practice for the students became a little stressful at times. We had run out of secondary schools in Uganda and so had to make use of schools in both Kenya and Tanzania. Some of these schools in all three territories were very remote. In many cases we had to supply the students with things like mattresses and tilly-lamps and to check their accommodation carefully. Each of us on the staff had an area where we were particularly responsible for the welfare of the students, but in addition we visited all the other areas so that the students could be advised and assessed as fairly as possible. It was hectic for all of us and involved much driving on very difficult roads especially if the practice coincided with the time of heavy rains.

As tensions rose in all the countries, travelling anywhere became difficult. My male colleagues were wary of letting me go off on my own and suggested we doubled up. But this meant one less supervision cover and I refused. In the event I had no real trouble though I did have to go through various road-blocks which were usually two large tree-trunks with spikes in them. On one occasion the guard moved only one tree and I drove over the other which did not do my tyres any good! But life went on, even when the army rioted. This had started in Tanzania. There came a time when British troops were sent for by Uganda. I well remember the important ministerial line-up at Entebbe Airport to welcome these troops, being left standing when the soldiers leapt from their plane and 'took' the airport!

Our Travelling Theatre

A happier story of travel which was trouble-free is the theatre we organised to go around rural Uganda. I had gradually become involved in the English language work which was an important focus for all the students. It became perhaps one of the most pleasurable parts of my whole programme. Because of my theatre interest I offered a drama module. We worked on a number of one-act productions which would be performed all over the country. This was following the initiative of David Cook and Betty Baker, Makerere colleagues who had established a student travelling theatre to be free for the people of Uganda and Kenya, and using a number of their languages. But because of the multinational nature of the student group we were able to do some quite exciting things. An Asian Sikh director might have an African assistant and an Irish stage-manager. An American drama major, directing a play in English, might have an Asian for his assistant and a Scot for his stage-manager, and so on. I joined the fun myself and produced 'The Bear' by Chekhov with a totally African cast. I had an American assistant and an Asian stage-manager. It was an amazing diversity, not only of language but also of cultural understanding and notions of theatre. We thrashed around, using the common language of English, and the frustrations were greatly out-balanced by the educative and enriching experience for all of us, not to mention the sheer enjoyment. We loaded our gear into a pantechnicon supplied by one of the aid agencies and set off into the wilds, stopping where the spirit took us. The reception was a great delight to us and worth all the effort. Most of the time these rural African folks would not understand the actual words as they probably spoke a language which none of our plays offered but they clapped and cheered as the message of the performance somehow got through. How marvellously across time and space, using the script of a skilful pen or its equivalent in oral cultures, can theatre present the universals of life and speak to the human condition everywhere.

Still with drama, and in the interests of demonstrating to the students the benefits and power of theatre in education, I had them helping the struggling drama group in a secondary school which was on the university campus. Here was produced one of the most vibrant and memorable 'Macbeths' I had ever seen. It was truly Africanised with the drums rolling and manifesting the universal nature of Shakespeare's work. The Africans love 'Shakespeare'.

Television Presenter

Which leads me into yet another memorable experience, for me at least. This was the part I played in Educational Television. Asked to do 'Drama for Schools' I had agreed with much trepidation when I discovered that a number of my colleagues had also been roped in. I had done a little radio broadcasting but television was right outside my experience. I was told that I would have to review a film of 'She Stoops to Conquer' produced for native English-speaking students and then write a commentary of my own which would be more suitable for those who spoke English as a second language. This would replace the original. I was given six programmes of half an hour each, to organise as I wished. I was writer, producer and performer. My scripts, done in advance and placed in a certain drawer for the typists to find, had a column for my commentary and one for the camera cues. This was all totally new territory for me and something of a nightmare.

The first problem came at the viewing stage. There was no quiet place for me to work. I had to watch the film in an office amid the clack of typewriters and general bustle. Then 'She Stoops to Conquer' had not arrived. Instead they had acquired 'Macbeth'. In a sense this was better for me as I was more au fait with this play. However the film was a film *about* it rather than *of* it, and I had to keep going back to make sure that my comments referred to what the students would actually see. It didn't help when the projectionist got the tins mixed up on one occasion and I had to help him to sort them out. They were not labelled.

Then came the day all too soon of my first broadcast. Nakasero Hospital had been converted into studios and these took the form of small bays around a vast room. I was there for my 'dry' runthrough in good time and watched with great interest a lady who had been seconded from the BBC, giving a presentation of Current Events. Would that I could have watched for longer. I was just beginning to learn from her when the lights on her bay went out and it was my turn. We never did finish the dry runthrough. It was time for me to appear and schools and colleges all over the country would be waiting for my pearls of wisdom! What a moment that was! I guessed that when the cameraman lowered his raised arm, I would be 'on'. And so it was. My face and all the preliminaries of the programme appeared on the monitor screen as I grinned into the camera and with a 'Good afternoon schools' launched into my script.

All my cues came from the cameramen who seemed to be thoroughly enjoying themselves mouthing Shakespeare's words along with me. There also seemed to be numerous by-standers in the shadows who were doing the same amidst other chat. Then, on that first occasion I was astonished to find children who had appeared from nowhere, perched up on a table behind me to watch the next bit of film when I stood aside. I had to shoo them off before I was due to appear again. I was fortunate to have a very able critic of all this in George at Mulago Hospital. 'You looked too much at your papers or at the monitor screen (I had explained everything to him), he would say. And what is all that noise in the background?' I duly reported on the latter and the large boom-microphone which picked up every minute sound, was removed. So ignorant was I of microphones that I did not recognise its replacement, a small gadget which 'you put upon your person'. I had no piece of outer clothing to which it would fix and while the technicians watched with great interest I attached it to my bra! Then came the time when I had a cold and took a coughing fit in the middle of the broadcast. I had to ask for a glass of water on the screen. As a result of this I nearly had a huge load of fan-mail. A European teacher I met said her girls had been most concerned for me. But it stopped there.

In the first four programmes I had covered the film. What now? Of course I could go from Drama as a literary medium to Drama as a performing art. So for the last two broadcasts I staged selected scenes, taking part myself and bringing in both Shimoni and Makerere students. I take my hat off to all concerned, including the resourceful television team who at that stage had had very little help from anywhere and yet managed to get the show up and running and to cope with the disgruntled academic amateurs who presented their programmes.

Teaching Journalists

During my time at Makerere I had another interesting 'outside' experience. I was asked by the Anglican church to tutor an English course in Katwe, a district of Kampala where they ran a mission. This course was to be for the journalists of the local papers who were writing in English as their second language or possibly third. They had their difficulties. I learned so much from them about the problems of operating in a foreign language, over and above what I had already gleaned from my teacher trainees. There is a factor which at one time was known as linguistic interference. It could manifest itself in some strange ways. For instance there appeared in the East African Standard one day, concerning the Grand Prix motor race, 'The drivers are closing their toes for the last leg'. I wonder if the reader can work this one out before continuing. It became quite a talking point for some time for those of us interested in language.

The writer was a Swahili speaker. It seems that in that language there is no word for 'finger' or 'toe'. You have to use the word for digit and then specify which limb it comes at the end of. The writer knew the idiom 'leg of the journey' and having used this he felt that toes would be more appropriate than fingers which came into the other idiom he knew, 'crossing your fingers' for good luck. But why 'closing'? He meant 'crossing' but had an l/r confusion in his pronunciation. Then he wrote it with one 's'. All very understandable when you think about it. Another story involving confusion of idiom tells of an African lady who had enjoyed a meal at the home of a European friend. As she was leaving she thanked her hostess by saying, 'That was a lovely meal. We are all very fed up'. I spent many interesting hours working from lists of typical errors so that I began where the students were.

Adventure in Kigezi

Just before I was due to go on another home leave, I had an adventure which meant more to me than perhaps any other I had in Uganda. One of my Shimoni African students, Charles Kabuga, the one who had lodged with the Bagchis, had come to Makerere to do further study. I did not teach him there but we kept in touch. I had been promising him for a while that I would visit his home in Kigezi. It was a long way and would require quite a bit of time out, so the adventure had to be carefully planned. At last, in May of 1964, an opportunity arose and I set out on a Friday afternoon, the car full of students' theses to be marked en route. I aimed to be away for a long weekend.

Kigezi lies in the southwest corner of Uganda, very near the borders of Congo and Rwanda. My way lay through Masaka and Mbarara, the road so far tarmacked and reasonable. I spent a night in the Tropic Inn in Masaka, one of the Uganda Hotels chain. There I worked on the students' theses both that evening and the next morning to the sound of the muezzin from a nearby mosque. I proceeded well as you often do away from home when any distractions cannot be for you. Then I continued my journey, stopping only twice, once for a coffee which I desperately needed at the 'Dysentery Arms', our nickname for a hotel run by a mad red-haired Englishman, the hotel having a doubtful reputation hygienically speaking, and again on the road, to lend a Sikh lorry-driver my spanner. I survived the coffee!

After Mbarara the tarmac stopped. On a red murram road I was now heading for the hills of Kigezi. The hinterland is gorilla country but I would not be going that far. I passed through the region of Ankole, whose cattle are very different from the beige, hump-backed variety in other parts. These are a dark, reddish-brown, have no humps and do have very long horns. The first sixty miles or so were not too bad but gradually the road got rougher and steeper. It twisted and turned like a scenic railway in a fairground, each bend revealing another magnificent panorama of mountains and valleys. I was conscious of many splendours but was unable to appreciate them fully as I had to concentrate on my driving. To make matters worse there were road works every so often, great bushes down the centre of the road, acting as bollards which had somehow to be negotiated. I dared not look at the terrifying drops. There had been no rain for months and red dust covered the car and me, especially if I got close to another vehicle. It became difficult to see.

But eventually I reached Kabale in one piece. This is the main town in the Kigezi area, where Charles taught in the High School. It was my immediate destination, a town with little more than a long straight High Street lined with dukas and all covered in red dust. I climbed the precipitous hill to the White House Inn, another of the Uganda Hotels. This was an attractive, spread-out building with the bedroom accommodation in separate houses and the lounge, dining and administrative areas in a central block. I registered quickly and after a glorious bath and a change of clothing, I lost no time in going to find Charles.

I was fortunate to pick up one of the school students in the High Street, so finding the place was no problem. Kigezi High was a boarding-school for boys. The pupils came from far and wide and Charles himself had been a student there and was now on the staff. I had just parked at the end of a large compound and the youth had gone off in search of Mr Kabuga, when I heard a shout. A waving figure was charging towards me. It was Charles, beside himself with excitement. 'I knew you would come and I knew it would be today,' he exclaimed gleefully. I had not told him when I was coming. In Charles' own little house I sat on the edge of his bed and drank beer and fanta and later had chicken and matoke, made from the plantain bananas, a delightful African dish, accompanied by the news of several months. Then came a request. Could I possibly teach some of the boys Scottish dancing? Charles had loved it at Shimoni College and had become quite an expert. Fortunately I had brought records for him and there was a school record-player.

'Some of the boys' turned out to be a hundred and twenty, virtually the school population! What a great evening that was, in the midst of which a startled headmaster appeared at the door! Who was this strange European woman and whatever was she doing with his pupils? He was soon happily taking part and a full-blown Scottish ceilidh was in progress. I left this joyous gathering regretfully with Charles making all kinds of plans for the morrow, Sunday. He would navigate me to his home, and bring others, relishing this unexpected opportunity for transport to take them home for a brief visit. It happened so rarely and public transport was non-existent.

So, next day, after European breakfast in the hotel and the warm African welcome of the night before when I shared 'Scotland', there now began for me a true highlight of my time in Uganda when I shared 'Africa' and loved every moment of it. There were in the car besides Charles and myself, one of the schoolboys, and Ezra and Philemon, Makerere students who were friends of Charles. Ezra's home was a place we could reach. Philemon came along for the ride. For about thirty miles the way lay along the tortuous road I had travelled the day before. We stopped before turning off on to a dirt track, for me to take some photographs of this unforgettable landscape. One or two local people stared in wonder. Charles told me that I was possibly the first white person they had been close to. Then we were off again, climbing and twisting and eventually stopping and walking to Ezra's home where the elderly parents were embarrassingly grateful to me for bringing their son. There was much talk in Ruchiga, Charles translating for me as I sat on a low chair and the others stood or sat on the floor. We enjoyed a pleasant, cool drink. This courteous hospitality was and still is typical of Ugandan homes.

Leaving the car on the track we continued our journey on foot. It was the only way from then on, a hike-cum-scramble. I was given a stick known as an enkoni, which I needed. All the Africans there carry them. We set out, one behind the other, Charles in the lead, I behind him, then the schoolboy and lastly Philemon. The boy suddenly darted off on a side-path to *his* home and the rest of us carried on to that of Charles. We shuffled along in the dust and the sun beat down. I could feel my neck burning. Up and down, in and out we went and eventually found ourselves amongst cultivated patches of maize, potatoes and sorghum. 'Mother is doing well', Charles said with pride. His father had recently died and Mother was the farmer. A vivid memory of this walk is the transformation of Charles. His shoes and socks came off and his

European tie, albeit it in the new Uganda colours, my basket went on his head and he became an African again, gloriously happy to be home. I was happy too both for him and with him. How I admired this man who seemed to be able to live easily and comfortably in three cultures, his own, the European culture of his education and the Bengali one of the Bagchis where he had found lodgings in Kampala. Had he any idea then, I wonder, of what he had really achieved?

We were approaching what I came to see as a kind of African Shangri-La, a 'lost' valley where it would be only too possible to drop out of the world. I was overcome by a sense of happiness and peace. Stopping on a ridge we looked down into a valley, in the centre of which was a number of small houses, wattle and daubed and thatched. 'There is my home' said Charles, breathing a big sigh of content. We were expected. The bush telegraph had been at work and members of the large family were coming to greet us. Also on the surrounding hills were clusters of curious but welcoming neighbours. It was not only the heat of the sun which was making me glow with warmth. Though nearly forty years ago, this glorious experience is as fresh for me now as it was then.

But the highlight of the highlight was my meeting with Charles' mother, Georgiana, surprisingly young, slim and attractive, in a blue frock and with her hair shaved as was the tribal fashion. We just gripped hands and loved each other on sight. Charles had long since mediated, speaking of her to me with great affection and pride and to her of me it seems in the same vein. So we knew each other already. Using his bilingual skills Charles continued now to mediate and to keep the conversation going. We were in Mother's house, each member of the family having her own. An older male relative joined us. He was wearing the kansu, that loose white robe which is the usual wear of the gentlemen and very sensible too in the heat. He was drawn into the conversation and much to our astonishment and amusement we discovered a shared experience. We had both had an operation recently for haemorrhoids! My friend had been very loath to leave his home and go to hospital but was finally persuaded to venture forth and when he returned cured and well, this did great things for Western medicine. I expressed the wish to see the banana shamba. Charles' mother took her panga, a wicked-looking knife shaped like a scimitar, and led me, barefoot and agile, along a hillside. I had some difficulty keeping up. Then she ran down to where her precious banana palms were clustered. I watched, intrigued, while she cut a large frond, twisted it into a rounded base on the ground

*The bananas **above** her head, Kigezi, 1964*

and then brought down a huge hand of the green plantain bananas which she placed on the base, lifting the whole on to her head. Without holding the bananas she then began to run home, with me in her wake and soon out of breath. My immediate ambition was to have a photograph of myself with this load on my head but I was warned that I might not be able even to lift it off the ground, never mind put it on my head. And so it was. See the photograph of Philemon holding the bananas just above me in the way that a minor queen at her coronation had the archbishop holding the heavy crown. What fun it all was!

Soon I was ensconced on a chair amongst the trees, with extended family and friends gathered round. Charles and I rendered Scottish songs and dances and the people clapped in time. Children who had begun to learn English were encouraged by Charles to show their prowess and came to recite to me. I was taken to the guest house and food was brought for Philemon and me, groundnut stew, matoke, and millet bread kept hot by leaves. It was delicious. There was also a pleasant drink. How quickly the hours flew by! I clung to the sacredness of that present moment, yearning to keep it for a bit longer. But we had to leave. As the growing procession of people gathered to walk us back to the car, I was suddenly presented with a magnificent live chicken. I *had* handled hens before in my limited farming experience and remembered to put the bird backwards under my arm but the protesting creature was not very happy to say the least and I was afraid it might wriggle its way to freedom and I would lose my present. But Philemon just quietly and expertly relieved me of it and we proceeded on our way.

As we approached the place where the schoolboy had gone off to his home, we heard some commotion. I was asked to go and meet this family and when we got into their compound we found people running about in all directions. A very fine cockerel which had been staked for a gift to me, had managed to escape and the race was on to recapture him. This was done and the cockerel presented to me in grateful thanks for bringing their lad. I felt quite overcome in more ways than one. Again someone kindly carried the gift for me and we continued on our way to the car. By this time there must have been more than a hundred people escorting us. Then, as the car came in sight, we saw Ezra and *his* family and neighbours. The crowd grew. Amongst this party was a boy with a badly suppurating knee. I offered to take him to the hospital. Somehow we all squeezed in. It was fortunate that my Peugeot was large and roomy. The boot was filled with farm produce, mostly tomatoes and Brussels sprouts. I turned in a very tight circle all the while calling out the Ruchiga farewell which I had recently learned. Gradually the emotive scene receded and we were on our way back to Kabale. I was on a very special kind of high.

A little way along the road, a goat suddenly leapt off the bank in front of us. I executed the most brilliant emergency stop that I had ever done! People bowed their thanks and I had a vision of startled faces and more waving hands. Back once more in Kabale without further incident, I took the boy with the sore knee to hospital, delivered the schoolboy and Ezra and my chickens (for safe keeping) to the High School and then proceeded with Charles and Philemon to Lake Bunyoni. There was an Anglican Leprosy mission here. I had met Grace, one of the missionaries, on the ship when I was coming to Africa, and I had promised to try and visit her. Now was my opportunity, as the place was not far from Kabale. It was good to have the companionship of Charles and Philemon which gave continuity to my wonderful day.

But the lake was very rough on that occasion as these African inland seas can often be. We had difficulty finding a boatman to take us, but eventually one fisherman agreed and we suffered a bumpy ride to the island. It was worth it to see the surprise and delight on Grace's face. She settled us on a verandah when the drums rolled for afternoon tea and we ate the traditional 'cucumber sandwiches' of the vicar's tea-party, or their equivalent, and drank very English tea. Charles had become European again but his splendid Uganda tie spoke of his homeland. What we talked about I cannot now remember. We did not move around, just sat there absorbing the atmosphere of this hospital in the wilds and enjoying the fellowship of interesting and intricate relationships. What greater joy can there be?

That evening in Kabale I met two of my Asian girl students who were visiting *their* families. Their fathers kept dukas. I was invited to supper in one home, and so I had a Hindu meal to add to my intercultural menu of the day and my tummy behaved splendidly! The day finished with a party in my hotel, African, Asian and European together. It was a fitting epilogue. In the morning I retrieved my beautiful chickens which Charles had put behind my seat in the car, with their legs tied. There was yet another emotive goodbye. I picked up the Asian girls and added their mountain of luggage to mine. I remember that we sang our way round those hairpin bends which were beginning to seem familiar, many of the songs useful for teaching English. I never lost an opportunity! The chickens lent *their* voices to the cacophony.

As the 'Dysentry Arms' came into view we decided that we must risk some sustenance. I had become attached to my chickens and I did not fancy doing what was expected of me and wringing their necks so I bartered them in this place. They were such excellent fowls, really valuable presents, that I did well. We got our meal on the house for one and for the other, I became the proud possessor of a miniature grain larder made in basketry. The roof comes off so I have a useful container with a lid. This was not new. It came from a home nearby. There were no tourist gift-shops in those days! But I valued it all the more as something from the people there and I still have it. We reached Kampala around five o'clock in the evening and I took the students home. This was one adventure it took me a long time to unwind from, mainly because I didn't want to. It had to be savoured like fine wine. It made me conscious of *my* particular pearl of Africa.

Chapter 14

Pointers to the Future

Home Again and Back

There was to be another intermission, another home leave, before I plunged into the last stretch, and my departure from Uganda. This leave was shorter than the last by about a month and it was summer in the UK though I cannot remember it being particularly warm! It was also characterised for me by two factors which stand out. The first was the change of family home. We now lived at 58 Newbattle Terrace in Morningside, quite near our old home in Springvalley Gardens. We had the top two levels of a four-storeyed house, the end one of a row. The terrace was a broad, tree-lined street, pleasantly quiet most of the time but with parking at a premium, especially when the cinema at the end was in session. It had no parking of its own. The nuisance of having to compete with the general public for our own parking space, however, was offset by the easy proximity to this attractive picture-house whose proprietor and owner we knew as he had been a neighbour in Braid Road. I enjoyed several films there with family and friends, during my leave.

Our elegant Edinburgh town-house was spacious and comfortable, except that there was no central heating. Mother was sure that this was not healthy! On this summer leave, I managed, but later memories are full of chill, particularly on the top-floor. Round the square which formed the first landing were the lounge, dining-room and one bedroom, also the kitchen and bathroom and a big walk-in cupboard. On the top floor were three other bedrooms, toilet/cloakroom and box-room.

My family, after about only a month in their new abode, were just beginning to know their neighbours. I was happy to introduce them to the Forresters opposite, the church people I had met in Nairobi, and through them to others with East African connections. The shops in the neighbourhood were also being explored. Dad, in his retirement, loved to shop around for bargains. With his little attaché-case, he became well-known and the shop-keepers enjoyed his banter. Later we were to be worried about his safety crossing roads. He suffered with glaucoma and lost the sight of one eye. But he carried on regardless.

Mother tried to keep up her stringent schedule of housework in spite of the many stairs. She would not have any home-help. Considering her varicose veins, I had been amazed that they had settled for this house so high up. But Mother loved it and as always turned it into a place full of love and warmth – of heart if not of physical comfort! It had a beautiful lounge, very large, with a huge bay-window over-looking the street. A lasting memory is of walking or driving to a point where I could no longer see the figure of Mother framed in this window and giving a last wave. The family had acquired a budgie called Dinky. He too was in the window. I was amused when I had to show my latest slides in Alex's bedroom so that Dinky would not be disturbed by the darkened room. For a short time at least we would share this home as a complete family. It was to be my permanent address for many years in spite of my travels and Dorothy's as long as my parents lived. Alex and Joan were to flee the nest after two years when they both married but Alex was already away much of the time as his work at Glasgow University made it necessary for him to continue to have digs in that city. So, the new home was a big factor of this leave as the change of church had been on my last.

The other thing dominating this intermission in my professional life was the change in me as a result of my work in the university, and how this seemed to bring me even closer to Alex. He had always had faith in my academic ability and was interested in my new work. He was also interested in thoughts I was now having about going for a university degree, though along with colleagues at Makerere, he did wonder if it was really necessary. I had 'got there without it' perhaps!

The leave as before gave me useful time for reflection. This really began when Alex and I went off in his newly-acquired car for a holiday in the highlands. The rest of the family had gone to Lucerne. I was able to share the driving and we covered some of the loveliest parts of Scotland, a highlight being our short stay in the Portsonachan Hotel on the banks of Loch Awe. Our visit co-incided with the engagement party of the Marquis of Lorne, a function complete with all the splendour of full highland hospitality and conviviality. Led by the piper the dinner-party marched in to the table, a colourful array of clan tartan, the men in the kilt with frothy white jabots and cuffs and the ladies in coffee-coloured lace gowns and sashes. Light from the chandeliers sparkled on the gleaming furnishings of the table and the piper continued both march and music as he circumnavigated the diners all through the meal. We also-rans dined in our own accommodation but the skirling of the pipes was our accompaniment too. My Scottish blood was up and I felt a real thrill to be a part of it all, even if the piper did stroll round the building again at the crack of dawn and I could think of gentler ways of being brought to consciousness!

Alex and I walked and climbed, and sat reflectively over picnics by lochs, reminiscing and sharing thoughts for the future. Alex suggested in the immediate term that I join him at the Burn, a place run by a commonwealth association of universities for academic retreats. As a member of a university staff I was entitled to do so. Not long after our return from the highlands then we went to this lovely old house, near Edzell in north-east Scotland. Set in spacious grounds on the edge of fine walking country, it afforded me more space for reflection. I was also able to do some writing and useful preparation for lectures.

I enjoyed time spent with Alex and his colleagues in Glasgow, too, including taking part in the university cultural life. At the university of Strathclyde I talked with a psychologist recommended to me by someone at Makerere and with nuns at the Notre Dame Training College for Teachers. I had another London trip and met with my professor there once more. He was helpful and encouraging, urging me to write another course for English teaching in East Africa in place of the present unpopular one. I also stayed for a while with Anne Godden of Nelson in whose flat I did some intensive writing of stories for their supplementary readers, a few of them based on traditional tales from my students. I was rewarded, apart from the publisher's payment, by Anne arranging a surprise party for me. She had managed to find several people we had both met in Uganda. And again I helped on the course for people going to work overseas. It had moved to Farnham Castle in Surrey.

So the weeks quickly and profitably passed. Back in Edinburgh I spent time with Moray House friends and former tutors and also shared my new experiences with my Gillespie's teachers, most of them now retired. There was a glorious sense of continuity in the midst of the whorl of new and developing strands. And one new piece of work which I greatly enjoyed was that of advising the Braille Press in their publishing of a book in Swahili. As before it was good to share all these exciting things with Mairi, our friendship picking up immediately from where we had left off. Little did we know that she had less then five years to live. She was to die of cancer at the age of forty. Her sister Helen who had shared that wonderful Lochnagar experience with us, had a breast off about this time. She also had cancer but was to live on into old age. I went to see Ena and her parents and Auntie Jean and Uncle Willie, now much better in health. Cousin Graham, their son, was now an enthusiastic Young Liberal. He was my projectionist again when I gave a talk/slide-show to his group. Joan was going steady, as we say, with Gavin and getting to know his family, and Dorothy also had a boy friend. It was a little later before we heard about Alex's Jane who had been one of his students.

Pervading memories of this leave are pleasant on the whole but marred by a consistent sore back which hindered me quite a bit. I was eventually able to find a doctor in Edinburgh who put me right but the trouble was to recur at various times in my life. Another black spot was the Vietnam war. The Americans had really got themselves and potentially the rest of the world at large, into trouble. We learned to sing, 'Where have all the flowers gone?' On a happier note the Queen had given birth to her fourth and last child, Prince Edward, and the Scots had built a road-bridge over the River Forth.

Finally Dorothy had her twenty first birthday party. The actual day was about a week after I would have left but she brought the function forward so that I could join in. In fact, if I remember rightly, I was the M.C. The party took place in a hotel and it was a very happy occasion. So I went out on a song as it were, with a great many 'advices and queries' to quote the title of an important part of our Quaker literature, buzzing round in my mind. Soon I was back at Makerere after a smooth journey, the only hiccup being that my luggage was left in London! It came on next day.

An Interesting New Project
I was plunged almost immediately into a venture which gave a great deal of interest, joy and satisfaction. A fellow educational psychologist,

Verona Harris, had discovered some young children in Mulago Hospital who were long-stay patients, suffering from polio. They had no education. Might we not do something to help? All this was very much by way of experiment. Verona had done the research and made the initial moves and I took over in the further negotiations and also in the teaching. The children were all of primary school age but it is doubtful if they had ever been to school or if they would have been even if well. They were from poor backgrounds, most from the bush, and there was no law at that time to say they must go to school. We saw this as a wonderful opportunity to give them some education. The big problem was of course the language barrier. None spoke English except one (see story below) and I did not have their languages, Luganda mostly. School work was limited to things done with the hands. I took paper and crayons and all kinds of material for making things. It is amazing how far one can go with signs and example. There were some quite astonishing results and a lovely feeling of empathy developed between the children and me through our silent communication. As the handicrafts were displayed and admired by hospital staff, the joy on the faces of the children was worth all the effort.

One day, by way of a change, I showed them one of my English teaching aids, a large poster with pictures of common articles on it such as a table, cup, knife etc. As I pointed to each the children said its name in their language. There was one little boy whom the nurses had not been able to speak with. He seemed to have none of the African languages they knew. In this session with my pictures I was suddenly conscious of something I recognised. It was the responses of this little boy. He was naming the articles in English! That was one language the nurses had not used. I was now able to say to them, 'Try English'. It seems that his mother had been an ayah to a European family, had left or died, and the child had been brought up along with the English-speaking children of the home. I am not sure of the details but it was a very unusual case, that this little African could be more comfortable with English than his tribal language.

I longed to tell the children a story. I managed to acquire a supplementary reader which went with a Luganda reading course. Luganda, like all the Bantu languages is 'phonetic' in the sense that the sounds and the marks on the paper have a close fit. I could 'bark at print'. Because I could read per se and understood the signposts like full stops and question marks, it was just possible that I could make sense of the text for my Luganda speakers. But first I must try it out on an adult bilingual. Who better than George? 'Yes', he said, 'you make sense', and he gave me a few tips. Excitedly I went to my school that day. The children were all over the room, most lying on the floor, engaged in their practical pursuits. I sat down in a corner and in a big voice began to 'read'.

Never shall I forget the effect of this. First one child turned and then another and gradually I had the riveted attention of all. They stopped what they were doing and began to gather round my feet, faces alight. From time to time they laughed. It must have been a funny story. It was difficult to glean its meaning from the illustrations which were small and insignificant. I held the children to the end when there was a moment of pregnant silence followed by an outburst of Luganda. This strange white woman had at last been able to communicate with her voice. But oh the sadness when they realised it was short-lived and somehow confined to this book! Child-like and particularly African child-like, they accepted the inevitable and went back to their handicrafts.

For me personally there was an amazing pointer here to the future. Twenty one years later when I was working for the British Council in Zambia I had to advise on reading policy in the schools. It became necessary to hold seminars for the people in the Ministry of Education, on the nature of reading. This experience in Uganda came to the fore and bore fruit. Just what *were* the skills involved in reading and how important was it to relate these to the experience of the reader? Much is common sense but sometimes it needs to be focussed upon. Of course I shared all this with my students at Makerere. They began to take an interest in the school and to assist. I was grateful as my time was limited and I needed help if there was to be continuity in the work. I began to look also for help from the African teaching force and eventually found an excellent lady. More of this below. Meantime, to my great joy, George was able to assist. His condition had improved to the extent that he was able to leave the iron lung for short periods. He could even leave the hospital provided there was a mobile lung available and a nurse nearby. He came to my school and taught arithmetic. This was a great day.

Taking George Home

Leaving the school for now, I must share another lovely experience. I managed to take George to see his mother. He had not been home since becoming ill and I doubt if his mother had been able to visit him. I picked him up on a Sunday morning. He was just being dressed when I arrived. He asked if I would take also his friend, a lad from Tanzania, who had had a lung operation. This boy rejoiced in the name of Heavenlight. With the help of the assistant matron we got the boys into the car accompanied by a nurse, and the mobile lung in the boot. Soon we were on the Entebbe road which led to George's home.

In all, the journey was about six miles. We had to leave the main road eventually and proceed on the murram. The house, a typical wattle and daub home, lay at the end of a very rocky path. I bumped and scrambled to the door. At first there were curious and even suspicious looks, but they quickly turned to smiles when George was spotted. In no time we were surrounded. I met his mother. She had no English or Swahili so, once again, communication consisted of smiles and hand-gripping, except when George had time to interpret. So many came to speak to him. The women wore the basuti, the attractive Baganda dress. It was very moving to see the pleasure George had in meeting his relatives and friends. Some thrust shillings through the car window. One dashed off to bring more neighbours. I got out of the car so that people could go in and talk with him. I was brought a low chair and I sat and looked about me. There was quite a sizeable shamba nearby with the inevitable banana palms. The whole African atmosphere of heat, colour and scent made its usual evocative impression on me, something I shall never forget. I was grateful to George for giving me the opportunity to experience it yet again in this very special way.

His mother changed into another basuti. I had asked if she would like to go to the lake, two miles away. This was a tremendous outing and merited a change of garment. When she joined us, I backed down the difficult path, my heart in my mouth, and we proceeded along the murram track till we came to Lake Victoria, sleeping in the midday sun. A few fishermen were working in their boats, and further out a white speed-boat shot across our view. Heavenlight exclaimed in awe and excitement. He had never seen Lake Victoria before, nor I believe, had George's mother.

I nearly wept. I was even more touched when, on our return to George's home, his mother gave me six eggs. I am sure her need was greater than mine but I accepted them gratefully. George received a huge pineapple and more shillings and Heavenlight was not forgotten. A neighbour's little girl, in the arms of her big brother, howled with fear every time I looked at her. She crawled up her brother's neck in her efforts to escape from the white ogre, and revealed a large expanse of shiny black bottom. The little children did not wear underwear. What a send-off we got! I was reminded of that in Kigezi. I picked up another lady and took her into Kampala too. She wanted to know how much it would cost. I daresay I might have done quite well in the taxi business had I been so minded!

Radio Lessons

To return to Mulago, it was about this time that I had contact with another school in the area. This was Mulago primary school, and it had nothing to do with the hospital. I had a friend, Beatrice Jones, who was a tutor in a training college for African primary teachers. She was writing a new course for them and had interested Radio Uganda. This body was anxious to offer in-service training to those teachers in remote areas particularly, who would find it hard to come to a centre. Somehow we all got together. Beatrice would write, I would offer demonstration lessons using children in a typical school and the radio people would broadcast. It was another pattern which proved to be a useful pointer to my future work. Mulago primary school seemed to be the kind of school we needed and the headmaster and staff were co-operative. So the project began. Beatrice fed me with the material. I dashed over to the school and used this with a selected group of children, and both of us filled our cars with them and went off quickly to Radio Uganda. It was a big adventure, fraught with frustrations. When the children were right the technical went wrong; when the latter was good, a child had a coughing fit and we had to start all over again. But it was fun too. The lessons continued in the car and our journeys were full of laughter.

One lovely memory which I cherish, concerning the school, is the time I came late for my teaching session because of university commitments and arrived to find the lesson in progress. Charles, aged ten, had decided they could not wait any longer and he took over. I stood outside on the verandah where I could not be seen by the children, and listened to myself in African guise, even to the Scottish accent! It was a salutary lesson from which I hope I benefited. Another memory is the Christmas party we gave the school as a kind of thank you gift for all their help. My students both Shimoni and Makerere came to assist. One of them in a Santa outfit borrowed from Draper's store, arrived at the crucial moment, ringing the school handbell. This was the only European part of the function. We were soon all dancing, African style, long lines of children and adults snaking in and out to the rhythm of the drums. It was a wonderful Christmas for all of us.

Adventure in Ankole

But some time before Christmas, a cheque arrived from Barclay Church in Edinburgh. This was in response to a talk I had given during my last leave. I had told the audience about Lillian, an amazing lady whom I had met when she was doing a course at Makerere. Her home was in the wilds of Ankole. Lillian must have been one of the first African feminists and was fighting a lone battle. She had started a Women's Guild and the place of their meeting needed a new roof. She had been able to name a sum and now, here it was. It was necessary for me to change it into local money and take it to Lillian. Ankole was a day's return journey by car. When I told Captain Kitney of the Katwe mission that I was about to go off into the bush again, he suggested I take Alan Jones, a lad from Voluntary Service Overseas (VSO) who had just come to work with him. I readily agreed. So it was that Alan and I set out early one morning on our four-hundred mile round trip, on not the easiest of roads.

I had only a very vague idea of where Lillian lived and worked. To get to Ankole was no problem and I *was* able to pinpoint to some extent when I reached this large area, but the final arriving took some time and many excursions to interesting places, including a meeting of a gombolola or chiefs' council. What this august body thought when they saw the solitary white woman (Alan had remained in the car) approaching their high-powered gathering, I just cannot imagine. Luckily for me there was some understanding of English and I was guided courteously and helpfully, though as I learned afterwards from Lillian, these male chiefs were very wary of what she was doing and might have looked on me as an ally of the enemy!

I tried to follow the guidelines I had been given and eventually, (I can see the spot so clearly in my mind), I had the strangest sensation of being near my goal. The road ran through thickly wooded country. A man was walking towards us by the edge of the trees. I stopped and said 'Lillian' in a loud voice. The gentleman stopped and spoke excitedly, waving his arms in the air, which seemed to indicate that he knew what I meant. I invited him into the car and continued cruising slowly on the way which my passenger had come. Suddenly the man made it very clear that he wanted me to stop, which I did. He headed into the trees and up the steep slope, again making plain what he wanted me to do. I had to follow him. Poor Alan! He was not sure whether to be more worried for me going off into the unknown or for himself, a non-driver, left sitting in the middle of nowhere.

My leader went at some pace. It was lucky that I was young and able. We came to a clearing and there was a lady busy with her cooking outside a small dwelling, with chickens running hither and thither. There was some conversation and then my guide turned abruptly and headed down the slope again. I could almost hear Alan's sigh of relief when we emerged. The man came with us once more and I had reached the point of thinking this cruising in the bush would go on for ever when we all spotted a lady in the distance but coming towards us. Once again my helper became excited and indicated that I should stop. He slipped quietly away when I ascertained that this was indeed, Lillian. I shall never forget the look on her face when I called her name. She took my guide's place in the car and promised to thank him properly for me. It had been Lillian's home I had visited with him and her mother to whom he had spoken. Now began for Alan and me a quite fantastic tour of other homes, including a kraal where we sat cross-legged with the mothers and babies, the children's eyes swarming with flies. Lillian told the women who we were and why we had come. The chorus of African 'Ees' and the hand-clapping were thanks enough.

I should have loved to stay longer. Lillian had so much to tell and to show us. But the day was far spent and we had a long way to travel home. I cannot even remember eating or drinking till we reached

Kampala again. Perhaps we had a picnic with us. I went at some lick, bad roads or not. Alan said that I did all the passing. Nothing ever passed me! I delivered him safely back to Katwe. It had certainly been a true initiation for him. And I went to a party at Mengo, though how I found the energy to be sociable I'll never know. Perhaps it was the feeling of mission accomplished that carried me through.

Back at the 'Ranch'

Lest it be thought that I had neglected my Makerere duties let me hasten to say that far from doing less there, I had in fact added to my load. A new B.Ed course had started and I was now teaching on that. The students here were mainly African. All my other course work and teaching practice supervision continued plus the many dramatic activities, so I had a very full working life. And the socialising with friends and colleagues widened and deepened perhaps all the more because of the uneasy political situation and the need for solidarity. At one stage I organised a Burns Supper, mainly for the staff and students of the faculty but friends from other faculties also came and it was a hilarious occasion. My African geographer colleague, Senteza Kajubi, brought the house down with his vibrant Toast to the Lassies. Once he

With some of the B.Ed. students, Makerere, 1964

understood that his task was to say nice things about the ladies, he was away, a gifted speaker with no notes at all. The Grand March and eightsome reel had to be seen to be believed, totally multicultural and gloriously chaotic. The famous Ally Anderson of the Scottish Country Dance Society and my former teacher at Gillespie's, would have had a heart attack. But surely there was a kind of universal love in this very Scottish affair. I hope Robert Burns was smiling in Heaven!

One particularly happy friendship which began for me when I was at Makerere was that with Dick and Gwyneth Drown. I met them through colleagues. Dick was principal of King's College, Budo, the 'Eton' of Uganda, and Gwyneth taught English there. I spent many happy hours at the school and at one stage went on holiday with the Drowns to Mombasa. I am still in touch with them in the UK. A fond memory is of a Christmas dinner at which seven members of the Makerere medical faculty were present, most of them surgeons. One I recall, was Birkett who gave his name to a famous tumour. An argument arose as to who should carve the turkey! Another memory is of watching a very English cricket match with cries of 'Well-played old boy' amid the measured clapping as the student batsman walked off the pitch. Again –what had we done?

Thoughts of our future amongst the Europeans in Uganda were never far away in the current political climate. There was an urgency in all of us to make a decision as to whether or not to stay on in the new Uganda. In my own case was the added dilemma of whether or not I should take time out to do a university degree. I had seen as a possible future line for me, work with the British Council, and had talked with one or two of their personnel. They gave me to understand that if I wanted to go in that direction, a degree was essential. Meanwhile, within the faculty my immediate colleagues, especially Professor Lucas, John Bright and Gordon MacGregor of the Language Department and Sentenza Kajubi who now had a high position in the faculty, were anxious to keep me for two particular reasons.

The first was my interest in speech training. I had tried out a few new ideas and they were kind enough to say that these were worth developing and might I write a course? The other was the notion of a new Institute of Primary Education. As the only 'expert' in the university in this field they saw me as playing a leading role. Then away from the university altogether, I was approached by the national school inspectorate and asked to join their ranks. So many options and so much that was worthwhile and tempting! I had need of my friends to help me to make decisions. I am grateful especially to Moira Harbottle, the department mathematician and to Verona Harris, also to Deryke and Audrey Belshaw, shipboard friends, and Margaret Macpherson, in the Theatre Guild, who were in other faculties. Then I still had contact with Ganesh Bagchi and his wife. All of these gave me wonderful support.

But of course the decision had to be mine. Perhaps the thing which tipped me towards taking time out to do a degree, was the knowledge that my friend Beatrice Jones of the radio project, was to do just that. She hoped to win a place at the new University of York and had applied to do a combined course of Linguistics and Philosophy. Should I try to join her? Could I move from the Senior Common-room to the Junior? York also had a combined course of Linguistics and English. Should I go for that? Robert le Page, the professor of Linguistics at York happened to come out on a visit. I am sure he must have had other business than to interview Beatrice and me but this he took on. He sat on the student side of my desk in my office and described his course. It was all rather dream-like. The upshot was that, subject to the agreement of the professor of English, he would accept me if I applied. I could start at York in the autumn of 1966. Eventually both Beatrice and I applied and were accepted. I had very mixed feelings but there was some relief in having made the decision. Also, there was the strong possibility that once I had the degree I would return and continue where I left off, all being well politically. Meanwhile there would be much tying up of ends. Someone who was particularly interested in my decision was Dr Sutherland of Moray House. He had come to Uganda on the invitation of the British Council as a VIP and I was honoured to have him and the British Council representative accept my dinner invitation. Dr Sutherland remembered me as his student at Moray House College. Speaking of VIPs, one of the assets of being a big fish in a small pool, as it were, was the chance to meet many interesting and well-known people. I have referred to another already. Hannah Stanton, Warden of the Mary Stuart Hall for women students, was a remarkable woman I am proud to have known. She suffered bravely in South Africa and was imprisoned for her stand against the policy of apartheid. I also met the wonderful Trevor Huddleston whose book, 'Naught for your Comfort' is an evocative name, and the novelist, Naomi Mitchison, another who came to dinner. But I must stop name-dropping and return to my tale and two memorable experiences in particular which brought me untold riches.

Christmas in a Leprosy Mission

The first of these came about because of my close friendship with Father Maguire, the Scottish Catholic chaplain to the university. He asked me if I knew anyone who would be willing to teach Scottish dancing to the pupils in a leprosy mission school some seventy miles distant from Kampala. I knew what he was really asking and I agreed to do it! I offered to spend a week of the Christmas vacation at this settlement, giving a concentrated course.

The St Francis Leprosarium was at Buluba, near Iganga, and it occupied some eight hundred acres of what had been tsetse infected jungle, on the shores of Lake Victoria. Elephant, hippo, wild pig, and crocodile had roamed at will and no human being could exist in the area. Gradually humankind and science conquered the fly and about thirty years before I went there the Franciscan nuns had established a small convent. People had begun to move into the region, many suffering from leprosy, and a hospital was begun. I had had several dealings with the Roman Catholic church and its work in Uganda, giving talks and advising generally in its schools and colleges. I was familiar with the White Fathers. But this was the first time that I had worked with the Franciscan nuns and the first time in a hospital. I was proud to be allowed to do so.

The settlement served a wide area, some of the outpatients living in special villages as far as a hundred miles away. The villages were visited regularly by the Field Sister. Other patients walked twenty miles weekly for treatment, and the constant coming and going of these people, many of them badly mutilated, was a daily scene at Buluba. There were some five hundred in-patients, with one European doctor (an East German lady) and seven dedicated sisters to run the mission. Apart from the priest who was Dutch and two ex-hunters who were German and helped with the maintenance, the staff of nurses and others were all African. Quite a large proportion of the patients were children so the mission had also to concern itself with education. A primary school had been established and facilities for carpentry, housecraft and farm-management had been developed. Large tracts of bush were being cleared for the planting of sugar, but already cotton, maize and cassava were cultivated and there were herds of cattle, both local and Guernsey, not to mention the various breeds of hens and ducks, special pride of one of the sisters. The young patients were taught to care for the animals and to help on the land. Many had plots of their own whose produce they could sell to the mission.

It was these younger patients with whom I was mostly concerned. I had been asked to teach the boys, as the girls had already been given a course in Irish dancing by one of the nuns. We used a hall situated near the men's wards, and during each dancing session, the windows were packed with interested spectators who sang and clapped in time with the music. Children who were unable or who did not wish to dance, sat round on benches inside the hall, while the toddlers ran in and out. It was a noisy, lively scene and not perhaps the best situation for teaching, but the enthusiasm of the learners made up for any deficiencies in other directions, and before long certain dances began to take shape. It was a valuable activity too as a bringing together of the community.

I found myself teaching also a few of the school teachers and some of the medical assistants. The ladies in this group were useful partners for the boys. Sometimes I was able to persuade reluctant dancers from the benches with fun things like the 'Elephant Dancer' or the 'Hokey Kokey'. So quite large numbers of all ages and both sexes became involved. I included a few action songs such as ' One Little Thumb' and 'The American Railway'. The constant repetition of the English words and phrases assured that by the end of the week my pupils were singing in English even if some of the words were not very recognisable as such.

We were asked to stage a concert at the end of the week and the nuns turned the event into a wonderful Christmas party. It was held in the lovely garden in front of the convent building. I was astonished at the number of visitors, mostly nuns and priests from near and far. All the ward patients who could walk or crawl, were there to support us. It was a colourful scene. In front of us Lake Victoria sparkled in the afternoon sunshine. The bougainvillea and the scarlet canna flowers contrasted with the rich green of the grass and trees, and on the verandah the sisters in their cool white habits glided in and out amongst the guests, serving tea and Christmas fare and generally looking after everybody. There was much laughter, and the glow of fellowship was as warm as the equatorial sun giving a temperature which seemed to soar to great heights. I was slowly melting in my Scottish tartan skirt and stole which I had worn for the occasion. Later, as I sat in the convent sitting-room, sipping a cool drink and watching the sun dip behind the hills across the bay, I was again filled with a sense of God's presence and peace, difficult to describe. And then, when I retired to the little thatched-roofed house I had been given for my stay, deep in the trees edging the lake, I felt at one with the hippos which stalked round my abode in the evening, snorting their pleasure in their perambulations, with the bats who lived above the netting on my ceiling, even if they did tend to smell a bit, and with the millipedes and geckos which also shared my living-room. As we say in Scotland, 'We're all Jock Tamson's bairns'. I wonder if God recognises His Scottish pseudonym!

But it *was* Christmas, and no account of my stay at Buluba is complete without something of the events on Christmas Eve and Day. I had expressed the wish to go to the midnight mass and I was made very welcome. At that moment I was not a Presbyterian, simply a Christian, happy to worship with my new friends. I even helped to train the sopranos in the choir item of 'Adeste Fideles'. The large church was packed, all ages present, babies sleeping on their mothers' backs. All, including the nuns, must have been tired. There had been a huge present giving earlier when the entire community had been catered for by these amazing women, even to garments lovingly stitched. The sewing and the gathering of toys and other gifts began each year as soon as Christmas was over. I was not forgotten either, nor any of the staff.

We left the church at 2.00 a.m. and over the mince pies served in the sitting-room, plans were made for me and another guest, the Reverend Mother's lay sister, to be taken by boat next day across the Buluba bay. We would be ferried by one of the ex-white hunters and our destination would be the recently built house of the other who was establishing a fishery for the community. The house would be an

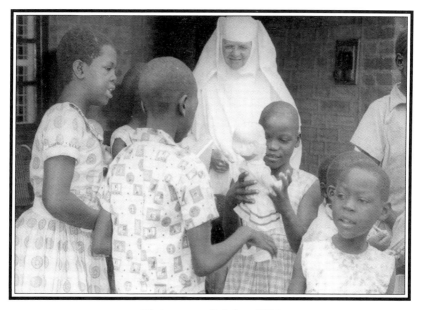

Christmas at Buluba, 1964

important base. We left early on Christmas Day in a small vessel with an outboard motor. The lake was not very kind to us and the little craft pitched and tossed. Fortunately my fellow-traveller and I were both good sailors. It was useful that we were carrying as cargo a large can of oil which was placed in the centre of the boat and helped our balance.

We received a big welcome in the German-style house. It was interesting to see that our friend had even made a stove-like ornament in one corner of the room in the manner of German homes at that time. He had also put a tree in another corner, not unlike a European fir. We had brought little gifts from the nuns and these were hung from it. Coffee was served and we were regaled with exciting tales of the wild. The men no longer hunted to kill, except for fish. But they sometimes shot crocodiles which emerged from the lake very near. There was the body of a six-foot one lying on the shore then. We were told that elephant came into the compound at sundown. As the afternoon lengthened into evening I stole wary glances outside but nothing came to disturb the quiet peace of this lovely place while we were there. Large birds of many colours perched sleepily on the stumps of the trees at the water's edge and the waves which had buffeted us out in the bay, now lapped gently against the reeds, the intense quiet broken only by the voice of our host as he held us enthralled with his stories.

Too soon it was time to go and we ventured lakewards once more. It was almost dark when we left. On one side of us the land was shrouded in blackness; on the other the disappearing sun turned the water of the lake to a deep ultramarine. We sped towards the settlement, the waters now peaceful. As we approached the darkened foreshore of the hospital there came the problem of finding a way through the reeds to solid land. Even the light of a lantern was not very helpful in the discernment of a path through the tangle. We jumped as four figures suddenly loomed out of the shadows and appeared like wraiths in a mist. They were four of the young patients. They had heard the motor of our searching boat and they had come to pull us into the safety of the land and the light. They led the way, once we had left our craft, up a winding path until we reached the lighted compound. As we were being led I was moved to consider that our guides were children being brought out of the darkness of illness into the wholeness and light of health. I gave thanks for this band of dedicated sisters and their staff whose work was hard and could still be fraught with danger. The possibility at that time of contracting the disease through constant exposure, was still there, before the appearance of modern drugs. I felt greatly privileged to have experienced this wonderful place and to have been able to serve it in a small way. I returned more than once and brought my students.

Worth Forty Cows!

Another memorable experience referred to came about through one of my TEA students who was a personal friend of Gordon Godfree, principal of a primary teacher-training college in remote Karamoja. The student had spent a vacation there and suggested my help and advice, subject of course to my agreement. I was only too happy to oblige as the mysterious Karamoja had long fascinated me. The difficulty was finding the time. My programme was already too full. I did however get in touch with Gordon, and found that he would welcome advice, particularly in the fields of infant methods and drama. The Indian lady, a Mrs Jignasu who was responsible for these subjects, was to go off on maternity leave. He himself would have to stand in. It was a task I would enjoy and I determined to try and *find* time.

It happened that I was asked to adjudicate the speech and drama festival at Namagunga, a girls' convent school near Mbale, which lay in the direction of Karamoja though a long way from it. Towards the end of term in April of 1965 I managed to arrange things so that I could combine this day of adjudication with an on-going trip to Karamoja. And so it came about. I spent Monday the 12th of April at the school adjudicating, and stayed at Mbale overnight after brief stops at Jinja and Tororo en route. I had looked forward, as always, to getting away and to the long drive on my own in the bush. I cannot explain this. I just revelled in the peace I found in the wide open spaces under the hot African sun. How I enjoyed reading Karen Blixen's 'Out of Africa'. I have read it more than once, with a deepening sense of empathy. I never felt lonely or afraid on my travels, just happy. Where I got this from I don't know. Maybe one of my ancestors was an explorer. But it is good to be alone sometimes, especially when most of the time people are clamouring for attention and help. I wouldn't have liked it all the time because I need people around me, but after a safari like this on my own I always felt strengthened and ready to give once more. From Mbale I went to Soroti where I had a quick coffee stop at the guest-house, booking myself in for a night on my return, after which I headed into the unknown. This was the rainy season and there had been an unceasing downpour all the day before. Driving conditions even on the tarmac were hazardous as the windscreen wipers could not cope. At one stage I had to stop in the middle of the road until the volume of rain eased, praying that nothing would run into me. Now, five miles out of Soroti, the tarmac ceased and there began for me a driving experience which I shall never forget.

But first, let me try to describe the region. It lies to the north and east of Uganda near the border with Kenya. It is a vast stretch of arid, sandy land where very little grows except scrub. The people at that time lived in the distant past. Most of them wore very little or nothing at all except perhaps a cloth slung over one shoulder. The women had a

Karamajong warrior

goatskin skirt hanging down behind and a little cloth in front. They wore bracelets and necklaces, beaded before marriage and metal when the bride-price was paid. Once on, these metal bands were never taken off, and if the women had to go to a dispensary or the hospital in Moroto, the main town of the area, the nurses found their necks moving with lice. They never washed.

There was a strong resistance to education and change. If electricity wires were put up, the people knocked down the poles and stole the wire to make those neck-bands, and also spears. They knocked down signposts too as they didn't want people to know where they were. Their language was harsh and their whole culture very different from any other in Uganda. They lived in close-packed villages, for protection against wild animals and marauding tribesmen. A good wife could cost as much as two hundred cows and very few young men could afford this, so they stole cattle from their neighbours much as the rievers on the Scottish/English border did in times past. It was now illegal to carry a spear but most houses contained them and the men were prepared to use them. We were continually hearing about another state of emergency as internecine warfare broke out, and there was more burning of homes.

Lion, leopard, hyena and many other animals roamed the land still and the place was rampant with snakes and scorpions. Water was the greatest problem. Rivers were few and their beds dry for most of the year, and bore-holes were expensive. Pumps had to be maintained. The people walked miles for water which was often full of disease-carrying microbes but they seemed to prefer this to the fresh water which would appear in the rivers after the rains. The latter was insipid and had no tang! The sparse growth was eaten by goats of which there were millions. Buildings cracked and eventually collapsed because of the sandy foundations, as their Bible should have warned the missioners who built there in the first place! Roads were impassable in wet weather and one could be cut off for weeks on end.

Thoughts of this were much in my mind as I ventured into this exciting new place. I wondered if I might have to be rescued by helicopter! When the tarmac road ceased I found myself slithering about in mud. I passed a slow-moving lorry, nearly ending up underneath it. From then on fortunately I neither passed nor met another vehicle as the road narrowed and became a kind of heaped-up viaduct crossing a swamp. A skid left or right would have meant a possible nose-dive into the ooze. I crawled in first gear at about ten miles an hour. My knuckles on the steering-wheel were white with tension. After hours of this anxious concentration I came on a solid concrete bridge with parapets of a kind. It was like an oasis in a desert. When I took my hands off the wheel they were shaking. I paused here until I could recover my nerve. This terrible road seemed to stretch into infinity in front of me and all the time the rain poured down over a landscape that was steadily becoming more and more dreary.

In a funny sort of way I was enjoying myself. It was a real challenge and a tremendous adventure. I had food and the usual safari gear so I knew I would be all right for a time even if I *did* get bogged down. Eventually the rain eased and the road became wider and firmer though strewn with rocks which were another hazard. I had crossed the swamp and was now in Karamoja proper. As conditions improved I was able to increase my speed and give some attention to the scene around me.

The vast plain was broken here and there by strange rock formations. Herds of goats were tended by small, naked boys, sometimes resting on their special Karamoja stools of which I later acquired four of different varieties. In the distance there were mountains. There were also clumps of stunted trees in parts and in the midst of these I met cattle with their herdsmen, one at the front and one at the back, naked men carrying long sticks. I had to stop and let the cows fan out round me, which they did with great curiosity and mooing. It was a weird experience just to sit there and watch this seething throng of animals passing me on either side. It was some time before I realised there was a man standing by my car-door. He stood there for a long time, desperately trying to make communication and I eventually joined in his efforts.

How I wish I had had a tape-recorder running! I now cannot recall the exact nature of our communication but it was quiet and courteous and I felt that we did make contact. It went on and on and the cows kept on coming. Then they stopped and my interlocutor left abruptly to join his fellow who had been bringing up the rear. I was able to continue my journey. Gordon, a geographer, had sent me an excellent map of his own making and I was able to pick out the landmarks leading to Lotome, the compound where the training-college was, all except the police-post which had been removed, as the latest state of emergency had subsided. This threw me a bit until the next landmark had me back on course. I had to turn right, off the road on to a track through trees. This was about seven miles from Moroto.

I met women and children with huge piles of sticks on their heads. They stood and stared or scuttled across the road in front of me. I was happy to realise that I had reached civilisation again. But the way still had other problems for me to negotiate besides the rocks and pot-holes. Gordon had marked three bridges and I duly crossed them though one did not exactly inspire confidence. I was now travelling over a mixture of sand and mud, dodging the deep corrugations as well as I could, sometimes having to leave the road altogether where it disintegrated into large pits. I passed a native village with its high stockade and closely packed huts. Then suddenly I saw ahead of me some white buildings. At the same time I saw a car approaching. I couldn't believe my eyes. I had reached Lotome and this was Gordon in his Volkswagen taking one of his students to Moroto. He kindly turned back to see me settled. I met his wife Christine and little boys aged four and two. I was to stay in their home. Thanks be to God. I had finally arrived. I was to be here for four days, having a taster of a life few Europeans would ever know, sharing the remoteness but aware that for me the experience was short and temporary. In the training college there were fifty students, learning to teach in primary schools. At one time there had been other Europeans on the staff but now only Gordon the principal. All the rest were Africans except for Mr and Mrs Jignasu, Asians who were second generation Christians. Both the Godfrees and the Jignasus were appointed while the place was still a mission. It had become government controlled but some funding still came from the mission. The Jignasus had two children who attended the junior secondary school which was also in the Lotome complex along with two primary schools. Mrs Jignasu had had several miscarriages. There was some concern that all would be well this time and that the weather would not prevent her from getting to the hospital. It was a strange life for these two expatriate families, completely cut off from their own kind, with no diversions whatsoever except what they could create for themselves.

Living conditions too had their problems, for example water and power. There was a village pump but it frequently broke down. Electricity was generated but the machine was expensive to run and very erratic It was used for only about three hours each evening and everyone retired early. Lighting most of the time was by oil lamp. Cooking was done on charcoal fires and calor gas and the pressing of clothes with a charcoal iron. A close watch had to be kept on the buildings for signs of subsidence. The Godfrees' bungalow had been recently built but already cracks were appearing in the walls. Gordon was then in the process of building a new house for the college cook. His bed had disappeared down a hole in the old one! The Godfrees had their dry toilet at the end of the yard. I was warned to look out for scorpions and snakes which tended to live there, especially a reptile called an Egyptian cobra. I never did meet any. Another loo hazard was that the structure had the habit of disappearing down its own hole! This had happened four times. Again I managed to escape.

The particular hollow in which Lotome lay was also subject to freak and powerful storms. Gordon had watched the entire roof of one of his classrooms just lift off and divide into two, one part depositing itself in the dormitory block and the other in the shamba. It cost the earth to get fundis (workmen) from Moroto, so most repairs and indeed building had to be 'Do it Yourself'. Gordon was teacher, administrator, doctor, plumber, carpenter and builder, all rolled into one, a quite remarkable man. And Christine too had to be a lass of many parts. She ran a sewing class for the women and made all the garments for her own family. She coped marvellously with the difficult water situation, wisely allowing herself to be guided by the local ladies, especially in the caring of her children. She also became an expert in first aid, even to administering injections. She kept serum in her fridge against snake-bite. My admiration for both Gordon and Christine knew no bounds.

But there were times when the situation could become almost beyond *their* enormous resources. Such a thing had happened just before my arrival. There had been a strange epidemic of meningitis amongst the students and two had died, one in Gordon's car! Sadly these two were from the same family, the father being one of the few educated Karamajong and one of two members of parliament for the region. In spite of his relative sophistication he was convinced that there had been neglect in the care of his sons. He blamed the staff, the European nurse in particular (perhaps that is why all the Europeans left) and threatened revenge. The Godfrees' bungalow had been turned into a fortress with screaming tribesmen chanting their war-cries and waving their spears. Somehow the police had been informed and arrived in time. There were no casualties. But how quickly in a closed, cut off community, things can get out of hand. Gordon and Christine played down their own part in all this but I suspect that cool-headedness and much prayer were the saving grace. On their CV's there should have been 'the ability to cope in crisis'.

It was unfortunate that because of my day en route adjudicating at Namagunga, I just missed the students at their classes in Lotome as term had ended the day before I arrived. I did, however, see their exhibition of teaching aids and watched their concert, performed outside and attended by the pupils and teachers of all the schools. The adults sat on the verandah of the dormitory block while the children sat below on benches clutching storm lanterns. I was warmed by a sense of community cosiness and fascinated as always by sharing in the things of another culture. It was particularly interesting to see the Karamajong dancing, so different from any other African dancing I had seen.

And I was able to fulfil my main purpose of going to Lotome, at least to some extent. Gordon and I discussed a great many things. He seemed to appreciate someone from the outside world being there. I hoped at that time to return later in the year to run an intensive course for the staff. Meanwhile the Godfree family were to be in Kampala at the end of that month while Gordon was doing a course in phonetics at Makerere, and we could continue our discussion then. Christine had never been to Kampala except when she first arrived in Africa. Apart from work I have some other vivid memories of my stay at Lotome. There was the day I went with Christine and the children to the local shops, three rectangular mud buildings with wide glassless windows. I was wearing trousers and the effect upon the locals was quite impressive! Christine knew enough of the language to understand what was being said. I was very slim in those days and comments were being made about whether or not I was a man or a woman! One group of lusty warriors who sported only large white feathers, stopped their energetic discussion to stare in wonder and follow with their eyes my progress into a shop. When we entered this shop a crowd gathered outside and some came in with us. Again I experienced the serious and courteous attempts of people trying to make conversation to which I responded with what I hoped was a friendly smile. The younger Godfree boy was asleep in his pushchair outside, surrounded by the ever-curious women who never ceased to advise Christine to put the child on her back. It is interesting that in modern times, Westerners *have* adopted this practice but probably more because of convenience than the importance of bonding which the Africans understood. The older boy sat on the shop counter while his mother made her purchases. He was relaxed and quite at home. Already he had picked up much of the Karamojong language, naturally and easily. It was an odd up-bringing for those two little ones but how wonderfully rich!

Another day, the weather being reasonable, we decided to go for a run towards Mt Moroto. We went in my car, it being more likely to hold us all and to cope with the road which was stony and full of pot-holes. We made good progress as we climbed, keeping a careful lookout for game. There was so much that we could have seen but we were unlucky until, on the way back, I suddenly spotted something moving near the side of the road. It was a greater kudu, a large antelope rarely found in Uganda and only in this area. In fact there were three of them. I longed for a photograph and we left the car to try and obtain one but our tracking skills were not up to it and the animals' camouflage was too good. We followed for a while then returned before losing sight of the car. It would be all too easy to get lost in that wilderness. The only other animals we saw were one of two orange-nosed dik-dik which scuttled off like lightning as the invading car approached. But we were thrilled with our kudu. It made the journey worthwhile.

We had lunch at a rest-house and then visited John Butler, headmaster of the new secondary school which was in process of building in Moroto. The stories of his difficulties, physical and administrative, made our hair stand on end. He lived in a new staff house, high up on a hill with an extensive view over the empty wastes beyond Moroto. The house *looked* lovely but already things were going wrong between walls and roof because of the shaky foundations. Also the builders forgot about cooking arrangements! And no furniture was budgeted for. While the school building was crawling upwards, John used part of an existing primary school, the road to which was impassable in the rains and he had to wade through the mud for two and a half miles there and back each day. The wind blew continually. Doors banged and nearly came off their hinges. Thick dust covered everything and John's office had to be dusted three times a day. He had nice beds for his pupils but no mattresses and only eight pillows at that stage. Officially and on paper, there <u>was</u> a secondary school in Moroto! But John seemed to thrive. When you are struggling for the means of existence, other pressures like exam results take second place so I suppose he was in no worse state than the heads of secondary schools in the UK.

On another occasion Gordon took me for a walk in the vicinity of Lotome. We went to see one of the villages. It was quite a long way in the heat. All that torrential rain I had experienced on my journey seemed to have been absorbed and everything was dry and dusty. The hard earth was baked and the silvery thorns shimmered and sizzled in the heat of the sun. We crossed an empty river-bed and there in front of us was the stockade of a village. We were soon surrounded by women and children, many of the latter herd-boys. Then suddenly a splendid figure emerged from the stockade, a very tall fine-looking man wearing an elaborate head-dress and little else. He bowed politely and soon Gordon and he were chatting. I turned away and became very interested in a nearby water-hole, but out of the corner of my eye I could see the gentleman looking me over. Eventually he bowed himself out and re-entered his stockade. We were not invited inside. 'What was all that about?', I asked as we continued our walk. 'Oh', said Gordon lightly, 'Our friend wanted to buy you'. 'And how much was I worth?', I went on with some curiosity. Gordon laughed. 'Forty cows', he replied, and added, 'The man knew that I already had a woman and that European men usually had one only so he reckoned that you were surplus to requirements'. I thought of the two hundred cows expected of a young man for his first bride if she were to be a good purchase and I accepted humbly that I was way down the line! Ah, well ! It is not given to everyone to know their true value.

My final memory of Lotome is a day with the Jignasus. First I went with them to Kangole, a little shanty town some distance away. I was reminded of scenes I had seen in films of the wild west. There was one long street with ramshackle buildings and saloon bar. Instead of American cowboys with six-shooters there were African cattlemen with clubs. We had refreshment in the back room of the one Indian duka which sold everything from sandals to Milk of Magnesia. In the evening of the same day the Godfrees and I had supper with the Jignasu family after which we had worship together. It was Good Friday and my last night with them. I started homewards early next morning.

As I returned across the swamp, the road now dried out and remarkably improved and the sun shining, my heart was singing and full of thanks, not least for the soundness of my vehicle and my safe travel in such difficult circumstances, but above all for the wonderful way in which such differing cultures can meet and love. This experience had been particularly poignant and Easter was very special for me that year. It was also a pointer to the future of another kind, as I was to have lots more experience in the years ahead of remote places and cultures, all over the world.

Chapter 15

The Last Stages

Mwanza – Last Teaching Practice Safari

Before bringing this first part of my life's journey to a conclusion, I shall record just one or two last-minute events and thoughts which seemed at the time to be of significance. To an extent they sum up much of my time in Uganda.

First, my final teaching practice supervision which took me to Tanzania, to Mwanza on Lake Victoria. The roads were particularly bad after recent rains and so it was necessary for me to fly and to pick up a car at the airport. A neighbour gave me a lift to the air terminal. The small bus took me and an African passenger to Entebbe where a DC3 was waiting, rather humbly parked behind an enormous VC10. We were a quarter of an hour late in leaving, but had a very smooth flight. It takes about two hours with fifteen minutes stop at Musoma, a remote air-strip in the middle of nowhere. The plane was rather like a country bus. As it trundled to a halt in front of the minute erection serving as the airport building, the waiting passengers were lined up as if at a bus-stop. Everybody knew everybody else and greetings were exchanged and playful banter. 'Come on Charlie. Let's get off. I've a date with a bottle of beer in Mwanza'. It was all great fun. There was an African stewardess who served coffee en route. We flew low for the most part over the lake, and occasionally had a few bumps as we hit air pockets, but it was much pleasanter than I expected.

In Mwanza I was greeted by a polite Asian, 'Miss Garvie from Makerere? Your car awaits you'. This was service. A brand new Vauxhall was at my disposal for the time of my stay. The man simply handed me the key and I drove him the three miles into the town. I must have passed muster as he gave me the necessary documents and left me to it. The hotel was right in the centre of Mwanza, a busy little fishing and market town, about the size of Kelso. I had four schools to visit, the furthest away being five miles from the centre of town. It was a tight schedule, as I had to supervise eleven students whose time-tables necessitated a hectic shuttle service for me. And I dared not drive fast as the roads around Mwanza were very badly tarred and if you went at more than thirty miles an hour you hit the roof. It was better on the murram.

I did manage to see everyone and three students twice, after careful planning of time. In addition, I spent two evenings at one school, running sessions with the Literary Society. They were studying 'Macbeth'. The students had given the game away about me and my TV series so the teacher asked me to help. It was all very pleasant and the girls were most responsive. They were thrilled apparently to speak to a Makerere lecturer who had also been on TV! My students were so welcoming and co-operative. When I arrived a letter from one was waiting in the hotel, inviting me to lunch the next day. I had most of my meals with them, at different schools. Some stayed with members of staff and some were given houses to share. They had settled in very nicely. The house where we had the meetings of the Literary Society stood high, overlooking the lake. Behind were strange outcrops of rock, a frequent feature of Tanzania. It is leopard and hyena country and the hyenas come right up to the door at night. This place really was the end of the trail, not very far from the town, but out on a limb and with an atmosphere all its own. As I drove home at about 10.00 pm numerous creatures watched me pass. I picked up the eyes in my headlamps. But when I slowed down to get a closer look, the eyes and their owners had vanished.

The hotel itself was interesting. Nearly all the occupants were, like myself, spending a few days on business of some sort. The dining-room was full of brief-cases. I spent the first evening in the company of a gentleman employed by 'Railways and Harbours'. Most of his working life had been overseas. He was fun to be with. As a sideline he did animal photography for Armand and Michaela Denis, a famous husband and wife team whose numerous adventures all over the world were often filmed. Another man I met was a Scot, manager of Coca-Cola for East Africa. I had encountered him on my first afternoon, out on the road when I was looking for a school. I slowed down to enquire, not sure if the man was Asian or European as he was very dark. A voice much more Scottish than mine said, 'I'm sorry I canna help ye lass. I'm a stranger masel. But what part o' Scotland do *you* come frae?' We had a good laugh later in the hotel.

There was so much to photograph. The lake was very beautiful there, with its fringe of palm trees, and the clothes of the fishermen and their womenfolk were bright and colourful. Monkeys played on the grass in front of my room at the hotel. They were very tame and quite oblivious of people. There was never a dull moment. With all of this plus work which was so interesting and rewarding, my memories of 'Mwanza' and indeed all my teaching practice safaris would live on through my years in York and long after.

On the final day I did some supervision early and then met my Asian friend at the hotel to complete the business of the car. I had over-stepped the mileage allowance, all on work. He drove me back to the airstrip. The plane was over half an hour late but I finished my reports while I was waiting. The return flight was rather more bumpy than that coming. We were served lunch in a cardboard box. I was ready for it by that time. I munched contentedly while the lake and its misty islands sped by below. Every now and then a water-spout shot into the air, a quaint reddish colour in the haze. Such land as we flew over was studded with hills and circular bomas of native huts.

When landing again at Musoma the plane came in quickly as there was no competition for air-space. A bell rang for the passengers to fasten seat-belts, and in a few minutes, just as I thought we might take a header into the lake, we bumped down on to the earthy runway and taxied up to the landing-stage. Entebbe seemed enormous when we finally arrived there. Most of the passengers were going on to Nairobi and as we were late, they didn't even check in but just jumped off the DC3 and on to the Friendship which was parked alongside. I returned to Kampala by bus and got a lift with some Asians to Makerere.

Business Unfinished and Completed

It very nearly happened before I left. I refer to the proposed Institute of Primary Education. I had written two papers on it and Senteza asked me to have them typed for discussion purposes. We then called a meeting of various people, some from the Faculty of Education and some from the Ministry, to talk about the development nationally of primary work. My papers, which contained a number of quite radical suggestions because of my very real concern about the general trends at that time, caused a few raised eyebrows. Unfortunately I never did hear the outcome of all this. It was a piece of unfinished business I was sad to leave behind. Something I felt much happier about was the hospital school. I have spoken of the African teacher we found to replace me. She turned out to be just right, and her salary was guaranteed by the municipal authority. So this bit of business was nicely completed. Interest in the school had grown and a royal visit planned, but Princess Margaret was unwell on the day so the visit was cancelled.

Another very positive memory is the last piece of work I did for KATS, directing the musical, 'Belinda Fair'. I have put together below, pieces of letters written home about it at the time. I was tempted to emend the structure and English but decided to leave them as they give the flavour just as it was. I have included the account at this last stage of my story because I feel it expresses and sums up not only my theatre work but the total essence of my Uganda years. So often and continuously I had felt the power of God's guiding hand.

I took over the stage direction from June who had lots of acting and singing experience but had never directed before, and she was finding the whole thing too much. I was not at all sure that I could do any better. I had never produced a musical or had to be concerned with elaborate historical costumes and changing scenes. We came to what turned out to be a very useful arrangement. June would look after the choreography and costumes which were her real interest and I would direct the movement. She was to be called 'Producer' and I 'Director', a double-act often seen but with a different connotation in film production. And we both worked closely with Frank, the Musical Director. We were a team. I suppose my own particular forte was 'discipline'. I didn't mind being a bully if I thought it was necessary!

"We're almost there. This has been a long hard week, with me driving over fifty people and myself along with them. Monday night was chaotic. The first act is extremely difficult, with lots of big spectacular chorus numbers, and the plotting of movement

has been a marathon task, but terrific experience. Tuesday and Wednesday, second and third acts, Thursday complete show, last night make-up and costumes and first act again till after midnight. I had been in the theatre from just after 2.00 pm except for an hour and a half at supper time, plotting the lighting and working with all the technical staff. And I made a student's class at Makerere at 8.05 a.m. this morning!!

Since Monday in particular, I have been conscious of a strength and ability that are not mine. I just know I'm being helped with this. It is affecting the whole production. The spirit completely changed from one of rather indifferent acceptance of instructions to one of complete co-operation and enthusiasm. We have an immense team now, working flat out. I've never experienced anything quite like it. My drama project up here had this spirit, but these were my students. The people I am working with now are other Europeans, most of whom I did not know, many of whom were suspicious of my methods and perhaps a little resentful of my bullying, especially the men, who are older than I am, in many cases. Men don't enjoy being directed by a woman. It's been the hardest fight I've fought, especially as musical direction was new to me, and I was breaking new ground. I've had many sleepless nights. But I felt on Tuesday that I had won the battle. One man asked me at midnight last night if he could come for extra tuition on his part. There is a feeling the show will 'go' now. We have some scenery up, a few colourful costumes in evidence, and the whole atmosphere is exciting and full of anticipation.

This is the theatre I love. I lose count of time. Yesterday afternoon I sat in the auditorium behind the director's desk with its special light, and nothing else existed except the show. The Technical Adviser sat with me, while we tried one effect after another. Spot-lights, battens, no.1 this and no.4 that were flashing on and off, bringing up to full light, dimming, blackouts, - the lot. I didn't realise how hungry and tired I was until I started to move.

During rehearsals people go about quietly while I keep my

eye firmly on the stage. The musical director is in the orchestra pit, call-girls bring the cast to their places. Members of the cast bring me drinks from time to time, while I watch my little pictures come to life. It's all so terrifyingly professional, and I can't believe I'm in command. People all over the place, including my colleagues and students, ask me how it's going. It seems that everyone is coming to the show. Students have appeared at rehearsals. My American drama student has come more than once, and he discusses it afterwards. I'm amazed at the interest and overwhelmed by the responsibility. The theatre seats are the same prices as at home.

I could go on and on. I'm eating, sleeping, dreaming – 'Belinda Fair'. Tomorrow morning (Sunday) I shall be in the theatre till lunch-time. Monday night is the technical rehearsal with the cast, and Tuesday is the full dress-rehearsal. I have had sessions on lights, sessions on music, sessions on acting. Now for the synchronisation! Let me tell you about my opening picture. I was excited by it last night. When I was discussing it (the show) with Angela Buse (professional), weeks ago, she said that if it were her show, she would open on a still picture, a Hogarth print effect. This would come to life with a bang. I have kept this idea in mind, but until I saw the actual scenery and possibilities of grouping, I wasn't sure I could create it. The show opens in the court of an English inn in 1702. There are trees all around, an inn court-yard and French window with steps, a rustic table and benches and a wall with trees over-hanging. An inn sign swings in true inn-sign fashion. It is very colourful and effective.

I'm opening with a dark stage, slow curtain, and gradual bringing up of light and music till a crash of the music department brings the whole picture to life. Dragoons in bright scarlet, village-girls in gay skirts and blouses, serving-maids with trays of beer tankards etc. etc. spring from various postures I have given them into action and into song. It ought to be effective. But it depends on the synchronisation and tremendous concentration by a great many people. For the end of the act, I'm reversing the process. The soldiers march off to the French war with lots of waving and singing, and the curtain slowly drops on a picture left on stage, with lights and music dimming. The picture, a little different, goes into its frame. I do hope it works. How I wish you could see it.

At the finish of the show, we can say our efforts were worth it. This has been a miracle, a real answer to prayer. No-one can tell me miracles don't happen now. A show of this size normally takes at least two weeks more than we had, to put on, and when you add to that the fact that the director was new to musicals, the producer inexperienced, the stage-manager had never stage-managed before, and about three quarters of the cast had never been on the stage until now, that I came into the picture very late, knew nobody, had a week off on safari, in fact had four and a half weeks to weld the team, sort out the chaos and start a-fresh, as it were – well, you see what I mean by a miracle. I have never had a more difficult assignment. There were times when I really felt like retreating rapidly. On one occasion I went to see the President, Angela Buse, to ask her to be prepared for a withdrawal of the show. I just couldn't see it going on in the time. She was all set for the committee to meet in emergency conclave, and she attended the next rehearsal. We decided to give it a day or two. Then we went on. We had reached the point of no return.

There was a sudden change of spirit last week. I prayed like I never prayed before. This was no coincidence. One of my colleagues up here had lent me a book about prayer, after a discussion I had with him in the common-room one day. We had been discussing how one's prayers become dull and stereotyped, and how we really don't have enough faith to believe in an answer. I learned a lot from that book, and I put it into practice. The results were evident to all though the reason was not. So many of the company have remarked on the thing that happened last Tuesday. They are puzzled by it. The contrast was so great. Quite suddenly we had a show. Everyone knew it, and everyone worked like they had never worked before. I know that I was not the only one praying. You were. Others in the cast were, but the way in which the answer came was such that I knew *I* had been answered. I had an atmosphere in which I could give of my best. Everyone was behind me, from the Musical Director to the man who worked the follow-spot. Each night last week we progressed a little further. I was able to pick out the essentials for concentration, my brain worked quickly and logically, I seemed to be possessed of untold energy. I leapt on to the stage to demonstrate and back into the auditorium. My eyes and ears were everywhere. The company listened and carried out instructions to the letter. New back-stage helpers appeared. Scenery was shifted slickly and smoothly. Painting got done. Properties and costumes appeared. Visitors watched rehearsals and told us we were going to have a good show. This encouragement put new heart into us. Suddenly we all realised we were enjoying ourselves. The professional photographer who came to the dress-rehearsal, said it was the best dress-rehearsal he had ever seen.

We had arrived by 12.30 a.m. I spoke from the stage to the whole company and wished them well. June and Frank each said their bit, and we went home with the tune of 'They are jolly good fellows' led by one of the cast, ringing in our ears. I just couldn't believe it. Then came the opening night. A beautiful bunch of flowers awaited me, sent by Beatrice. Pushed under my front door, earlier, was a note from the Wilkins, university friends, wishing us well. We had an almost full house, even for that early performance, and a most appreciative audience.

The show went with a bang. I was almost in tears with joy and relief. The Press were there. You'll see our crit later. The Wilkins were there and we talked about it. I do enjoy their comments. They knew what I had gone through, and they thought it was a wonderful show. For all four nights, I walked about at the back of the balcony, just outside. I died a thousand deaths, as I saw things the audience didn't see. The cast watched my face anxiously at every interval, and I tried to cheer and encourage them all I could. They were like children. 'Sorry about that line', 'I was in the wrong place – did you notice?' I usually had, but the time of reproof was over. There were bits of temperament here and there. A hundred and one things to sort out and oil to throw on troubled waters on stage and behind, but the team spirit stood the strain, and we reached our final night unscathed, with congratulations pouring in on all sides.

A large car with Union Jack flying brought the British High Commissioner last night. House-full notices were up both then and the night before, and people were sitting on the steps. My opening picture got a wonderful round of applause. June had done a marvellous job on the costumes. It really was a blaze of colour. At times, everything was held up in the comedy bits, while the audience rocked with laughter and clapped the lines they enjoyed. I sometimes went away on my own and sat on the stairs or leant over the banister, weak with relief and my heart so full, I just couldn't have spoken to anyone. It can be a lonely job, being a director.

At the final curtain, June and I went on the stage. Each of us got a lovely bouquet. The leading lady also received flowers. When the curtain came down for the last time, we all remained on the stage, and Angela made a speech of thanks. June and I each received a beautiful cut crystal dressing-table bowl with inlaid silver top and musical figurine, and Frank got a silver cigarette case with his initials on it. The stage-manager also got something. I was left to the last, and Angela kissed me as she said her thanks and good-byes. She was crying and I felt awful. The company cheered and sang, 'For she's a jolly good fellow'. I was completely overwhelmed. Frank, who is reckoned to be a difficult man to get on with, is looking forward to my return and wants to work with me again. Louise, in the chorus, a girl going to York, is determined to be in my production there. We hear there is a lively dramatic society.

We had a whale of a party in the theatre foyer. One man after another bought me a drink. The young ones brought records. There was dancing and singing and lots of laughter till after 3.00 a.m. I slept till 10.40 this morning. So ends 'Belinda Fair'."

The cast of 'Belinda Fair', 1965

Au revoir Uganda

And so, in a sense, ends Uganda fair. I shall not linger on the emotiveness of the numerous goodbyes and endless parties. Perhaps the most difficult was my parting from Mary, my housegirl who had replaced Thomas. Somehow we had become very close, especially since I had acted 'taximan' when her nephew was born, going back and forth to the maternity ward with numerous relatives. The baby's middle name was Alexander, after my father. Mary, holding the child in her arms, was amongst a large crowd of people seeing me off at the station. There were friends of all races there. As the multicoloured sea of waving arms receded into the distance and the train gathered speed on its way to Mombasa, the waving seemed to be taken over by the fronds of the banana palms. I fancied I heard them whisper, 'You'll be back again. You'll be back again'. And they were right. I did return in a physical sense but spiritually, I never left the country. In all the years between, the Uganda factor was present. The story of my starting on that BA degree and then jumping to a Master's, must wait for the next book. It was the focussing which led to a wider field (see Chapter 12), the key which opened a whole new horizon for me. And it was in Uganda that this key was forged, Uganda in which I found my pearl of great price.

A Special Tribute
Uganda 2002

The Grand Pearl Hotel, Kampala

Forty years on I returned to meet my ex-students and their families and I stayed in this small hotel on Tank Hill. Charles Kabuga, Paul Mugumbwa and David Kiyaga Mulindwa received me into their fellowship as though the turbulent Uganda years between had never been. We had all travelled far in more ways than one, to many corners of the globe. And in their case, they had gone from the depths of national tragedy and depression to the present ethos of recovery and hope, in spite of the AIDS scourge which is still rampant but now better contained. It was a long time since we had shared that something special at Shimoni Teacher Training College. The college still exists and still functions. It is known today affectionately and proudly as 'the mother of all colleges'.

Thank you to my 'boys' for their love and care of an old lady, steeped in nostalgia, and thank you for confirming the conviction, grown through the years, that the Uganda and especially the Shimoni 'factor', has influenced everything which followed for me and has still never left me. In light of the message of this life story, the name of the hotel where Charles arranged for me to stay, is very significant. As we gathered and talked within its beautiful garden, we all had a feeling of having come home. My thanks, not only to the 'boys' but to their wives and children. They have given me a further treasure-trove of memories. May God continue to bless them and their lovely country.

Edie Garvie
Peterborough, U.K. 2003